LINKING THE LANGUAGE STRANDS

THE MANAGEMENT OF A COMPREHENSIVE LANGUAGE PROGRAMME

Published by Heinemann Education, a division of Reed Publishing (NZ) Ltd, 39 Rawene Rd, Birkenhead, Auckland 10.
Associated companies, branches and representatives throughout the world.
www.reed.co.nz
www.henz.co.nz

This book is copyright. Except for the purpose of fair reviewing, no part of this publication may be reproduced or transmitted in any form or by any means, electronic or mechanical, including photocopying, recording, or any information storage and retrieval system, without permission in writing from the publisher. Infringers of copyright render themselves liable to prosecution.

While every care has been taken to trace and acknowledge copyright, the author and publisher apologise for any accidental infringement where copyright has proved untraceable. They would be pleased to come to a suitable arrangement with the rightful owner in each case.

ISBN 1-86944-944-4

© 2004 Jill Eggleton and Jo Windsor
The authors assert their moral rights in the work.

Printed in China

Distributed in Canada by Harcourt Canada Ltd.
55 Horner Avenue
Toronto, ON M8Z 4X6

Customer Service
Toll-Free Telephone: 1-800-387-7278
Toll-Free Fax: 1-800-655-7307

Distributed in the Republic of Ireland by Carroll Heinemann
Unit 17-18
Willow Road Business Park
Knockmitten Lane
Dublin 12
www.carrollheinemann.ie

Distributed in Australia by Harcourt Education Australia Ltd.
22 Salmon St
Port Melbourne
Australia 3207

CONTENTS

Introduction	4
Linking the Language Strands	5
Language Processes	6
Oral Language Programme	7
Written Language Programme	22
Spelling Programme	85
Visual Language Programme	97
Organisation of the Classroom Environment	116
Organisation of Time	119
Conclusion	122
References	122

INTRODUCTION

"Students should be able to engage with and enjoy language in all its varieties and understand, respond to and use oral, written and visual language effectively in a range of contexts."
(New Zealand English Curriculum)

In order to achieve this aim, it is essential that the organisation and management of learning environments is purposeful.

A well-organised and managed language programme and resource is essential to help students develop in literacy.

Linking the Language Strands provides practical ideas for assistance in organising and managing literacy programmes in the classroom.

LINKING THE LANGUAGE STRANDS

In order to be truly literate, students need to be experienced in the three strands of language: **oral**, **written** and **visual**. Within these strands are the sub-strands of speaking, listening, writing, reading, presenting and viewing.

Growth in one strand will lead to growth in another.

Providing a balance in oral, written and visual language ensures that students of different learning intelligences are catered for.

The following chart gives an example of learning intelligences and their characteristics.

Type	Likes To:	Is Good At:	Learns By:
Linguistic	read, write, tell stories, talk	memorising names, places, dates and trivia	speaking, listening, visualising
Logical	do experiments, figure things out, work with numbers, ask questions, explore patterns	maths, reasoning, logic, problem solving	categorising, classifying, working with abstract patterns/relationships
Spatial	draw, build, design, create daydreams, look at pictures/slides, watch films, play with machines	imagining things, sensing changes, puzzles, reading maps, charts	visualising, dreaming, working with colours, working with pictures
Musical	sing, hum tunes, listen to music, play an instrument, respond to music	picking up sounds, remembering melodies, noticing pitch and rhythm, keeping time	rhythm, melody, music
Kinesthetic	move around, touch, talk, use body language	physical activities, sports, dance, acting	touching, moving, interacting with space, processing knowledge through bodily sensations
Interpersonal	have lots of friends, talk, join groups	understanding people, leading others, organising, communicating, manipulating, mediating conflicts	sharing, comparing, co-operating, interviewing
Intrapersonal	work alone, pursue own interests	understanding self, following instincts, pursuing interests and goals	working alone, individualised projects, self-paced instruction

LANGUAGE PROCESSES

In all language areas it is important to be aware of the language processes.

A prime objective in today's world is to teach students how to think critically, creatively and analytically.

- **Thinking** in diverse ways must be an integrated part of all language learning. Becoming literate involves reading and writing beyond a literal, factual level.
- **Exploring and learning about language** makes the student's implicit knowledge about language explicit.
- **Processing information** provides an opportunity to observe and assess the student's understandings.

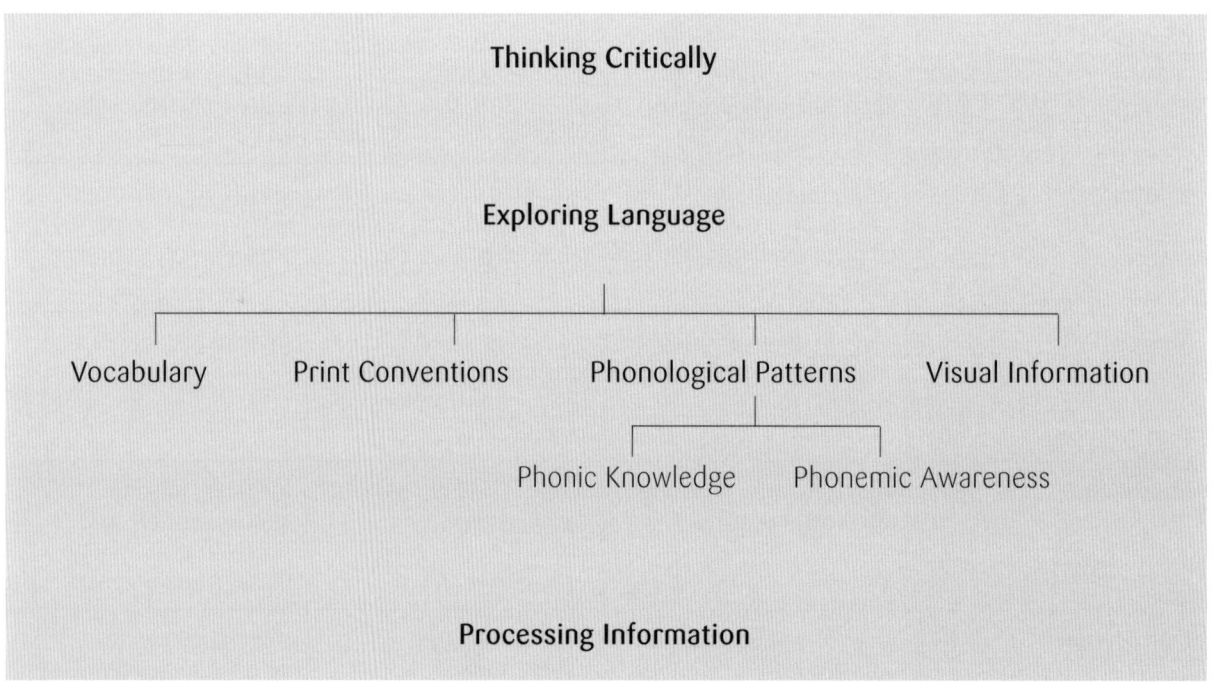

ORAL LANGUAGE PROGRAMME

The oral language programme is divided into two sub-strands:

1. **Listening**

2. **Speaking**

SUGGESTED LEARNING OUTCOMES

1. Listening
- To listen and respond to others.
- To listen and respond to instructions and directions.
- To identify some verbal and non-verbal language features (such as body language, gesture and voice modulation).
- To be able to make judgements about messages received.

2. Speaking
- To join in group and class discussions.
- To be able to tell a story.
- To be able to recite.
- To be able to read aloud.
- To be able to use the voice effectively, incorporating:
  - good voice projection
  - good expression
  - modulation.
- To use technology to enhance presentation and audience understanding.

OVERVIEW OF THE ORAL LANGUAGE PROGRAMME

1. Listening

Teacher Targets	Methods
To provide a programme that encourages all students to participate in listening activities.	By listening responsibly to partners. By listening to others in small group and whole class discussion.
To encourage students to be responsive listeners.	By providing regular, consistent opportunities to listen in a responsive environment.
To encourage students to value listening as a component of communication.	By giving students opportunities that require them to listen to oral language.
To enrich and extend vocabulary.	By having an enriched language programme.
To listen to a variety of oral language forms in appropriate situations.	By listening to different forms of oral language — interpersonal listening (listening to others) and listening to texts.
To encourage students to listen to voices being used effectively.	By listening to stories, recitations, poetry and the "reading to" component of language.
To provide opportunities for students to listen to a variety of speakers.	By inviting visitors to the classroom on a regular basis.
To encourage students to listen and respond, using a variety of questions to generate thoughtful discussion.	By listening to good models of questioning (literal, inferential or interpretive).

LINKING THE LANGUAGE STRANDS | NEW REVISED EDITION

Student Targets

These are the specific achievement objectives.

Emergent Stage (Level 1)	Early Stage (Level 1/2)	Fluency Stage (Level 2/3)
Interpersonal Listening	**Interpersonal Listening**	**Interpersonal Listening**
Students should: Listen to a partner. Listen in a small group. Listen to shared experiences. Listen to simple instructions. Listen to simple descriptions. Listen to responses to questions. Listen to opinions. Listen to others who are using personal drawings when giving messages.	*Students should:* Listen to a partner and ask appropriate questions. Listen in a small group and ask appropriate questions. Listen to others talk about experiences. Listen to simple instructions and follow them through. Listen to descriptions. Listen to questions asked of a speaker. Listen to opinions and reasons given by others. Listen frequently to the use of an enriched vocabulary.	*Students should:* Listen to a partner, question and respond. Listen in groups of various sizes, question and respond. Listen to recitations. Listen to ideas presented to small and large groups. Listen to more complex directions and carry them out. Listen to concise descriptions. Listen to responses to appropriate questions. Listen to and respect opinions and reasons. Listen to others who are using technology to present information. Listen to an extended and enriched vocabulary.
Listening to Texts	**Listening to Texts**	**Listening to Texts**
Students should: Listen to a retelling of a story. Listen to poetry. Listen to texts and make connections to personal experiences.	*Students should:* Listen to the retelling of stories both factual and imaginative. Listen to texts and make connections to personal experiences and written texts.	*Students should:* Listen to poetry. Listen to texts, identify the purpose of the text and recall and respond to the main ideas. Listen to texts and make connections to personal experiences, written texts and world issues.
Approximate Age Band 4–5 years	Approximate Age Band 6–7 years	Approximate Age Band 8–10+ years

Note: Age bands are broad indications only. Students develop at varying stages. Stages of development, not age, must be the first consideration when planning.

2. Speaking

Teacher Targets	Methods
To provide a programme that encourages all students to participate in speaking activities.	By conversing with partners, in small groups and in whole class discussions.
To encourage students to be confident speakers.	By providing regular, consistent opportunities to speak in a responsive environment.
To value speaking as an effective communication form.	By giving students regular opportunities that require the use of spoken language.
To enrich and extend vocabulary.	By having an enriched literacy programme.
To encourage students to speak in a variety of oral language forms in appropriate situations.	By giving students the opportunity to experience interpersonal speaking (speaking with others) and using texts.
To encourage students to adapt their speaking to different audiences.	By telling stories, reciting and reading aloud.
To encourage students to develop questioning strategies to generate thoughtful discussion.	By providing a variety of audiences for students to converse with.
To encourage students to use technology to enhance their speaking.	By giving students opportunities to use a range of technology to make oral messages more meaningful.

Student Targets		
These are the specific achievement objectives.		
Emergent Stage (Level 1)	**Early Stage (Level 1/2)**	**Fluency Stage (Level 2/3)**
Interpersonal Speaking	Interpersonal Speaking	Interpersonal Speaking
Students should: Speak to a partner. Speak with a small group. Speak about personal experiences. Give simple descriptions. Express an opinion. Ask questions using *how, why, when, where, what*. Begin to widen spoken vocabulary.	*Students should:* Speak with a partner and ask appropriate questions. Continue to ask questions of a speaker, increasing questioning strategies. Express an opinion and ask purposeful questions. Continue to use a wide vocabulary. Talk about experiences in a small group. Give simple directions. Give descriptions with some detail.	*Students should:* Speak with a partner/group, asking literal, inferential and interpretive questions. Tell personal or imaginative stories. Present ideas to small or large groups. Give more complex directions and instructions. Give clear, concise descriptions. Ask appropriate questions of a speaker to clarify meaning. Express an opinion and give multiple reasons. Use a more extensive and enriched spoken vocabulary.
Using Texts	Using Texts	Using Texts
Students should: Retell a story. Recite simple poems. Use picture books and personal experiences to give added meaning to oral messages.	*Students should:* Retell a story, both factual and imaginative. Read aloud to others. Recite poems. Ask questions during and after reading texts. Express an opinion and ask purposeful questions. Continue to increase spoken vocabulary.	*Students should:* Read aloud informally and for an audience. Tell and recite stories. Recite longer poems. Present or perform a variety of different text forms.
Approximate Age Band 4–5 years	Approximate Age Band 6–7 years	Approximate Age Band 8–10+ years

PURPOSEFUL LISTENING AND SPEAKING

Oral language is an integral part of the learning programme across the curriculum. Students need to have purposeful interaction using oral language. It is important to allocate times that provide students with different types of oral language experiences.

Interpersonal Language

Interpersonal language consists of general interactive discussion. It can be:

- Personal: e.g., *Last night I ...*
- Transactional language (language that is specific and functional): e.g., describing how to play a game, giving directions.
- Poetic language: e.g., describing a favourite character, retelling an imaginative story, talking about fantasy characters.

Using Texts

Using texts consists of the use of written texts to enhance oral language, such as books, poems, newspaper articles, Internet and personal writing.

ORGANISATION AND MANAGEMENT OF THE ORAL LANGUAGE PROGRAMME

The organisation and management of oral language needs to include a variety of formats:

1. Partner format
2. Small group format
3. Whole class format

1. Partner Format

The Organisation

- Put the students into a circle.
- Ask them to turn and face the person next to them (this person will be their partner).

Note: Change the partners daily.

The Discussion *(approximately three minutes)*

- Partner One shares information.
  Partner Two listens.
- Partner Two shares information.
  Partner One listens.

The Sharing

- Students return to whole class circle and face each other.
- Teacher asks: *Who would like to share what their partner told them?*

  Student: *My partner was Jack. Jack said ...*
- Teacher asks: *Who has a question they would like to ask Jack?*

  Encourage the students to ask questions that use the words *how, when, where, why, what*. (Discourage questions that require just *yes* or *no* answers — closed questions.)
- Repeat the process (no more than three times).
- As the children become more confident, introduce comments.

  Teacher asks: *Who has a comment to make about what you have heard?*

Management Points

- Change partners daily.
- Change topics frequently.
- Ensure the students sit in a circle facing each other when they return to the whole group.
- The format should include three shared messages and three questions on each message.
- Add three comments about the message once the above pattern has been established.

Weekly Management Board Guide
(use Monday to Thursday)

Stage 1

Place discussion ideas on a management board one week in advance, so that the students are aware of the discussion topics.

Stage 2 (as the students become more confident)

Use the management board as for Stage 1, but the topics remain for one or two weeks.

Note: Students must feel comfortable about sharing a message. There could be times when a student has a personal message that is very important to talk about. The student needs to feel they can share this, regardless of the topic.

Examples of Topics for Partner Discussion (Stage 1)

Exchanging Personal Information

Share with your partner:
- what you do when you get home from school
- people you know
- family
- places you have visited
- what your favourite time of day is
- what you like to do at home, at school, on holiday
- things you like/dislike

Recounting Experiences

Share with your partner:
- what you did in the weekend
- what you did on your last birthday
- what you did on holiday

Expressing Opinions

Share with your partner:
- what you think about television programmes
- what you think about food
- what you think about animals

Describing and Explaining

Share with your partner:
- how you get to school
- a game you like and how to play it
- how to make something

Stories

Share with your partner:
- a book you have read
- a story you have heard

Imagination

Share with your partner:
- what you would do if you had wings

Building Self Esteem

Share with your partner:
- some things you're good at
- something you like about your partner

Examples of Topics for Partner Discussion (Stage 2)

Topics could extend to connect with the reading and writing forms the students are working with, e.g., personal recounts, narratives, reports, explanations, descriptions, procedures, opinions.

2. Small Group Format

At the beginning stages of oral language development, it is better to have the students in partner or whole class formats. As they become more fluent, confident and responsible listeners and speakers, they can work in a small group format.

The Organisation

- Divide the class into small groups (five to six students in each group).

The Discussion

- Assign specific roles to each student. Introduce the roles one at a time, so that the students can become very familiar with the task associated with that role.

Specific Roles for Explicit Daily Oral Discussion

Manager	Manages the group.
	Watches time.
	Makes summaries.
	Makes sure the group understands the task.
Encourager	Makes sure everyone has a turn.
	Asks members to respond.
	Offers positive comments on ideas.
	Encourages others to participate.
Reporter	Reports group ideas back to the class.

Add the following roles when small group discussion is used in content areas, e.g., social studies, science.

Recorder	Writes down ideas.
	Asks questions to check understanding.
Observer	The observer can be either a new class member or a student appointed to observe the roles of other group members.

Small Group Format Ideas

There are a variety of ways to use small group formats to stimulate discussions.

Creative Clusters (an example)

- Divide the class into groups of five.
- Choose a manager.
- Give the students a topic, e.g., common experience, retelling a familiar story.
- The students speak around the group, starting with the manager.
- At 15-second intervals, the teacher indicates it is time to change to the next speaker.
- The last speaker concludes the retelling.

As the students become more confident with this format, encourage imagination in retelling, e.g., change the characters of the story, change the setting.

Debates

When the students reach the Fluency stage of oral language, debating can be introduced.

Choose two debating teams: For and Against. The rest of the class are observers. Each debating team has:

> Three Speakers:
> - 1st (leader)
> - 2nd
> - 3rd

1st Speaker: Speaks twice — at the beginning, to introduce the debate and present the arguments, and at the end to sum up (no further information can be introduced).

2nd and 3rd Speakers: Present their arguments.

Observers: Listen to the presentations and prepare a response stating which team has won the debate and giving reasons for this choice. The reasons need to refer to the delivery as well as the content.

Note: The students need time to prepare and practise before the presentation of a debate.

3. Whole Class Format

Whole class sharing is an integrated part of the class programme. Opportunities should be given for the students to share voluntarily during the day. Speaking formally to the class does, however, require a degree of competency.

When students are confident, formal speeches can be introduced. It may be necessary to provide students with a supportive framework for preparing a formal speech on certain topics.

For example:

About Me
- name
- where/when born
- something about the place where you were born
- where you are now
- school
- likes/dislikes
- family — something humorous
- interests/ambitions

News
- country
- location of country (map)
- something of interest about the country
- current news
- why this happened
- consequences (opinion)
- outcomes

A Smash Hit
- name of group
- where originated from
- make up of group
- style
- why a smash hit (opinion)
- future for the group (opinion)

Character Clues
- where/when born
- about birthplace
- where now
- why character is famous/important
- how became famous
- family (if significant)
- future for character

It Happened Last Night ...
- where (local area)
- about area
- current point of interest
- why this happened
- results
- future consequences

Go and See This!
- name of film
- setting
- era (description)
- plot
- what you liked/disliked
- characters
- scenes
- something memorable

Strategies to Promote Discussion

Plus Minus Interesting

Format

Step 1
Teacher provides a problem, e.g., dogs on public transport.

Step 2
Students suggest positive and negative aspects of the problem and raise interesting related ideas, under the headings plus, minus and interesting.

Step 3
Students develop a concise conclusion based on the discussion.

Plus minus interesting is a strategy that can be used with either whole class or small group organisation.

Problem: Dogs on Public Transport		
+	-	Interesting
keep owners company	no room for people	what about other animals
no dog sitter needed	people allergic to dogs	what about a public transport system just for dogs

Whole Class

When using this strategy with the whole class:

- The teacher acts as manager — organising the class, providing the problem.
- The students respond orally.
- The teacher records the students' responses.
- The teacher supports the students to develop a concise conclusion based on the discussion.

Small Group

When using this strategy with a small group:

- The teacher appoints students in the group to be the manager, the reporter and the recorder.

- The teacher provides the problem.
- The manager organises the group.
- The students respond orally.
- The recorder takes notes.
- The group develops a concise conclusion.
- The reporter shares the conclusion with the whole class.

Note: This activity is fast-paced and lasts approximately 15–30 minutes, depending on the developmental level of the students.

Storytelling

Storytelling benefits oral language development. It enhances oral language skills and adds an extra dimension to literacy, fostering creativity and imagination. Teachers need to model storytelling to the students and encourage them to become active storytellers.

Suggestions for Telling a Story

Before the Telling

Select a familiar story with a strong characterisation.

Internalise it.

Keep it short.

Memorise the opening and closing lines.

Practise.

If necessary, use notes to help you remember the structure.

Telling the Story

Concentrate on the story, letting the story do its work.

Keep the story moving without interrupting the flow.

Collaborative Reasoning

This is a strategy to improve the quality of classroom discussions.

Learning Intention: to encourage dialogue and reasoning skills among students after reading a story.

Steps

- The teacher reads the story.
- At the conclusion of the story, the teacher begins discussion by asking a question intended to provoke students into taking a position on an ethical or moral dilemma arising from the story, e.g., *Do you think Cinderella should have allowed the fairy godmother to make her into something she wasn't?*

Assisting Oral Language Development

Giving and Receiving Messages

It is important that students be given clear instructions on giving and receiving messages.

The following chart can be used at the beginning stage of oral language development.

When I am speaking I must:

Look at the audience.

Speak clearly.

Put my hands in my lap.

When I am listening I must:

Look at the speaker.

Listen carefully.

Ask my questions clearly.

The following chart can be used at a later stage of oral language development:

To give a good message I need to:

Look at the audience.

Use my voice clearly.

Make my voice reach the listeners.

Remember not to speak too fast.

To receive a message I need to:

Look at the speaker.

Listen carefully.

Ask about things I don't understand.

Retell the speaker's message.

Write down parts I might forget.

Quality Questioning

It is important for students at all levels to formulate questions that initiate and sustain discussion. The following chart shows examples of quality questions.

Knowledge

Where did ... ?

What was ... ?

Who was/were ... ?

Name the ...

Comprehension

What does ... mean?

Give an example of ...

Describe what ...

Application

What would happen if ... ?

If you were there, how would you ... ?

How would you solve this problem?

Analysis

What things would you use to ... ?

What other ways would you ... ?

What things are the same/different?

What excited/saddened you?

Synthesis

What would it be like if ... ?

Pretend you are ... Describe this.

How would you approach this problem?

What would happen if ... ?

Evaluation

What do you think will happen to ... and why?

Is this situation real? Why/why not?

What do you think will happen now? Why?

Select the best part of what you have heard. Describe why you chose it.

WRITTEN LANGUAGE PROGRAMME

The written language programme is divided into two sub-strands:

1. Reading

2. Writing

SUGGESTED LEARNING OUTCOMES

1. Reading
- To be able to select and read a wide range of text types, e.g., fiction, non-fiction and poetry.
- To respond to the way language is used while reading for meaning.
- To be able to identify some conventions of writing and aspects of the organisation of texts that affect the way we understand what we read.
- To be able to identify and question the meanings in written text, drawing on personal background, knowledge and experience.
- To be able to use a range of strategies associated with Emergent, Early and Fluent reading.
- To be able to use written texts as sources of information.

2. Writing
- To be able to write regularly to record personal experiences.
- To be able to write descriptively on a variety of topics, experimenting with language and form.
- To be able to write straightforward instructions, explanations and statements of fact in a range of contexts.
- To be able to identify and use some conventions of writing that affect the way we read text.
- To be able to write for an audience.
- To be able to plan, retrieve and present information in a variety of ways.

OVERVIEW OF READING PROGRAMME

Teacher Targets	Methods
To establish a balanced reading programme.	By reading with, to and by students daily. By providing a range of written texts.
To create a love of reading.	By showing enthusiasm.
To encourage students to respond to language and meaning in texts, developing an understanding that reading for meaning is paramount. To help students to use comprehension strategies.	By helping students make connections with text by forming hypotheses, asking questions, making inferences, creating visual images, identifying the author's purpose, summarising, analysing and evaluating.
To teach students processing strategies — how to solve unknown words.	By encouraging students to attend to the details of text, to decode and determine meaning, to predict, cross-check, confirm and self-correct.
To enrich and extend vocabulary.	By listening to stories, by interacting and role-playing experiences.
To recognise and cater for individual needs.	By regular monitoring (running records, observations, conferences).
To give students time to select and read a range of texts for enjoyment and information.	By having a timetable that allows time to read.

Student Targets
These are the specific achievement objectives.
Emergent Stage (Level 1)
To be able to listen to stories and recall some details.
To be able to retell a known story in sequence.
To interpret pictures and use pictures to predict text.
To be able to demonstrate the front, back and spine of a book.
To have correct directional movement.
To have one-to-one correspondence.
To be able to demonstrate the first and last part of the story.
To be able to recognise capital letter and lower case correspondence.
To be able to show a letter in a word.
To be able to recognise a capital letter.
To be able to recognise the difference between a letter and a word.
To be able to recognise some high-frequency words.
To be able to recognise some initial letters — names and sounds.
To be able to recognise similarities in words.
To begin to use some processing strategies: <ul><li>looking for information in illustrations, diagrams and photographs</li><li>looking for known letter/sound relationships.</li></ul>
To explore new books and return to favourite ones.
To show a desire to read independently with familiar material.
To be able to make text to self connections.
To be able to interpret the meaning of some visual information in texts.
Approximate Age Band 4-5 years

Student Targets

These are the specific achievement objectives.

Early Stage (Level 1/2)

To be able to attend to the details of a text, decoding and determining meaning by:
- focusing on letters and letter clusters
- identifying known words
- looking for information in illustrations, diagrams and photographs
- using increasing knowledge of onset and rhyme to work out new words.

To be able to identify words and anticipate what might come next by:
- drawing on letter/sound knowledge and patterns of text
- sounding out the words or parts of words
- using meaning to help
- rerunning text.

To be able to cross-check, confirm and self-correct by:
- drawing on meaning or patterns of text
- using illustrations/photographs and word knowledge
- rereading a word, phrase or sentence
- deciding if the text sounds right and thinking about meaning.

To choose to read more frequently.

To explore books independently.

To cope with more characters and scene changes.

To cope with a greater variety of text forms.

To choose to reread favourite and new books.

To increase the number of high-frequency words automatically recognised.

To increase phonic knowledge.

To improve flow and phrasing and increase reading pace.

To be able to make text to self connections.

Approximate Age Band 6–7 years

Student Targets
These are the specific achievement objectives.

Fluency Stage (Level 2/3)

- To be able to use processing strategies of attending and searching, predicting, cross-checking, confirming and self-correcting quickly, confidently and independently.
- To be able to form hypotheses about a text.
- To be able to make inferences from text and illustrations.
- To be able to differentiate between different text forms.
- To understand the structure and features of a variety of text forms.
- To be able to compare styles and forms.
- To be able to identify the author's purpose.
- To be able to summarise a text for retelling.
- To be able to create mental images, or to picture what is happening in a text.
- To be able to make a personal, informed response to a text.
- To be able to recognise the main idea and identify relevant supporting details.
- To be able to differentiate between fact and opinion.
- To be able to recognise the use of comparison and contrast in a text.
- To understand what is meant by action and response.
- To understand the meaning of cause and effect.
- To understand plot development, character development, setting and its relationship to the plot in narrative texts.
- To have a knowledge of literary devices, e.g., simile, metaphor, imagery, personification, alliteration, rhetorical questions, onomatopoeia.
- To have a knowledge of design features in a text, e.g., layout, headings, captions, maps, cross-sections, illustrative text, index, table of contents.

- To be able to read silently.
- To be able to read with accurate flow, phrasing and pace.
- To be able to maintain meaning over longer and more complex structures.
- To be able to cope with more complex characters.
- To be able to cope with less predictable texts.
- To choose to read for enjoyment as well as information.
- To respond to what has been read in various ways, including critically.
- To be able to generate questions.
- To have a wide interest word vocabulary.
- To know how to use resources to get information.
- To know how to use the library.
- To be keen to extend reading interests.
- To expect books to be a part of daily life and to seek time to read.
- To know how to set a purpose for reading.
- To be able to make text to self, text to text and text to world connections.

Approximate Age Band 8-10+ years

ORGANISATION AND MANAGEMENT OF THE READING PROGRAMME

The management and organisation of the reading programme will depend on the developmental stages of the children and the class numbers. A comprehensive literacy programme uses a balance of approaches:

1. Shared reading
2. Guided reading
3. Independent reading
4. Reading to students

1. Shared Reading

"Shared reading is an essential component of a daily literacy programme."
Effective Literary Practice, Learning Media

Shared reading can be used with a group or a whole class. The focus in *Linking the Language Strands* is on shared reading as daily, whole class interactive sessions.

Shared Reading Using Rhythmical Texts

In this shared reading session, the whole class gathers in the teaching space to read together a text that is rich in language, has a rhythmical pattern, a chunk of rhyme, can withstand repeated readings and is appropriate to the interest level of the students in the class.

The text for this purpose can either be:

- an enlarged book
- a suitable text on overhead transparency so that the whole class can see it easily.

Teacher Targets

- To use a rhythmical text to model correct enunciation, pronunciation, flow and phrasing.
- To convey to students the joy of reading.
- To extend and enrich the students' vocabulary.
- To encourage the students to think critically.
- To introduce and reinforce print conventions.
- To introduce and reinforce phonological patterns.
- To encourage the students to use and interpret visual information in texts.

Student Targets

- To become familiar with the rhythm, sound and patterns of language.
- To experience and foster a love of reading.
- To understand how to read aloud with flow and phrasing and dramatic interest.
- To increase and enrich vocabulary.
- To learn to think critically about the text.
- To practise reading aloud, attending to all print conventions.
- To use and interpret visual language in texts.

Suggested Format

One book is used over a period of a week.

Grouping: Whole class

Time Slot: At the beginning of the reading block before guided reading.

Duration: 10 minutes per day, Monday–Thursday. One hour or more on Friday.

Note: It is important that the story retains its flow and that interruptions are minimal. The main focus should be enjoyment.

Monday

Focus — Thinking Critically: Comprehension

- Introduce the story. Focus the students' attention on the cover illustrations and build eagerness and a sense of anticipation.
- Encourage the students to think critically about the story contents.
- Read the story, asking predictive questions only where appropriate, without interfering with the flow and enjoyment of the text. At the conclusion of the reading, ask the students questions that will generate thoughtful discussion about storyline, characters and setting. Include both literal and inferential questions.
- Encourage questions and comments.

Tuesday

Focus — Exploring Language: Vocabulary

- Revisit the same text.
- Encourage the students to join in with the repetitive language throughout the text.
- Focus on clarifying vocabulary as the words occur in the reading, encouraging suggestions for other words that mean the same.

Wednesday

Focus — Exploring Language: Print Conventions, Visual Information, Fluency

- Revisit the same text.
- Look at the first one or two pages and focus on the print conventions that affect the way we read.
- Find all the visual information in the text, e.g., bold font, increases in type size, illustrative font.
- Encourage the students to join in with the reading of the entire text, practising these conventions and "reading" the visual information appropriately.

Note: Each shared book will reinforce many different print conventions. Select those that are most appropriate to the developmental stage of the majority of students.

Example

Beginning Stage	Later Stage
full stop	possessive apostrophe
capital letter	parenthesis
comma	colon
question mark	semi-colon
quotation marks	dash
exclamation mark	ellipsis

Thursday

Focus — Exploring Language: Phonological Patterns (Phonic Knowledge/Phonemic Awareness)

- Revisit the same text.
- Read the entire text together without pausing and with enthusiasm and vitality.
- At the completion of the reading, use one or two spreads to focus on phonological patterns.

Note: Select those phonological patterns that are most appropriate to the developmental stage of the majority of students.

Example

Beginning Stage	Later Stage
initial consonants	suffix: -ly
blends	short/long vowels
suffixes: -s, -ed, -ing	prefixes
compound words	singulars/plurals
contractions	homonyms
word families	synonyms
rhyming words	antonyms
	word families
	word derivations

Friday

Focus — Processing Information
- Reread the text together.
- Discuss with the students the features of the text.

Example

Plot	Characters	Setting	Theme
Discuss how the story begins, develops and ends.	Major Minor	How is this conveyed?	Discuss and compare to other stories.

- Use drama or role-play to act out the story or parts of it.
- Respond to the story using written and visual language.
- Present the students' responses, either by making another book or as a wall display.

At the end of the week, the shared book and culminating activity become part of the independent reading resource.

Examples of Responses to Shared Books

Shared Reading Using a Focus Poem

In this shared reading session the whole class gathers in the teaching space to read together a poem that can easily be committed to memory. The poem should be appropriate to the *interest* level of the students in the class.

The poem is presented on a large card so that all students are able to see it easily.

Teacher Targets

- To promote and foster a love of poetry.
- To help the students become familiar with the elements of poetry: rhyme, rhythm, the sound of the words, word order, meaning.
- To encourage the students to read poetry aloud with flow, phrasing and dramatic interest.
- To increase and enrich the students' vocabulary.
- To engage the students in conversation about poetry and help them to think critically.

Student Targets

- To enjoy listening to poetry.
- To appreciate sound, rhyme and rhythm.
- To gain an understanding of the elements of poetry: rhyme, rhythm, the sound of the words, word order, meaning.
- To be able to discuss the meaning of a poem and think critically about it.
- To discuss conventions used in poetry.
- To use and interpret visual language when reading poetry, e.g., bold font, illustrative font, changes in type size.
- To understand how to read poetry with fluent phrasing and dramatic interest, both individually and chorally.
- To commit some poems to memory.
- To increase and enrich vocabulary.

Suggested Format

Select a poem to be used over a week

Grouping: Whole class

Time Slot: At the end of the writing block or another appropriate time, but not directly before or after using a shared book.

Duration: 10 minutes per day, Monday–Thursday. Approximately 30-35 minutes on Friday, depending on developmental stage.

Note: It is important that the first experience with poetry be enjoyable.

Monday

Focus — Thinking Critically: Comprehension

- Introduce the poem.
- Discuss the title and the poet. Using text cues, ask the students what they think the poem could be about.
- Read the poem to the students.
- Discuss the message and encourage the students to think critically about it, asking questions that will generate thoughtful discussion.
- Encourage the students to ask questions about the poem.

Tuesday

Focus — Exploring Language: Vocabulary

- Revisit the same poem.
- Read the poem, encouraging the students to join in.
- Clarify any vocabulary, encouraging the students to think of other words that mean the same or could have been used instead.

Wednesday

Focus — Exploring Language: Print Conventions, Visual Information, Fluency
- Revisit the same poem.
- Focus the students' attention on the print conventions or any visual information in the poem.
- Encourage the students to read the poem together, paying close attention to the print conventions and visual information that affect the way the poem is read.

Thursday

Focus — Exploring Language: Phonological Patterns
(Phonic Knowledge/Phonemic Awareness)
- Revisit the same poem.
- Read the poem together.
- Use the poem to introduce, reinforce or examine any phonological patterns that are appropriate.

Friday

Focus — Processing Information
- Read the poem, encouraging the students to respond to the rhythm in some way, e.g., clapping, stamping, thumping.
- Try to say the poem in a different way, e.g., make a tune for it, say it like a chant or a rap.
- Provide a blank book for each student. Paste a copy of the focus poem into the book and allow the students to respond in some way, e.g., at the beginning stage, students might simply draw on their own visual response to the poem. At a later stage, students could respond in a variety of ways, depending on the message of the poem, e.g., the poem may lend itself to a focus on alliteration, onomatopoeia, descriptive language, imagery, metaphor, simile or personification. Each response should be enhanced visually.

Shared Reading Using a News Book

Suggested Format

Prepare a large book made from blank paper. Each day the teacher adds a news item, e.g., for first and second years, add two or three sentences gained from oral interaction with other students. For following years, use information sourced from oral interaction (personal news) and newspaper and magazine articles of high general interest.

Grouping: Whole class.

Time Slot: At the beginning of the day.

Duration: 10 minutes per day, Monday–Thursday.

First and Second Years

- Reread previous personal news items at pace (no more than seven items).
- Reread the news items together, demonstrating processing strategies if a word is unknown.
- Use comprehension strategies — ask questions (literal and higher order), ask the students to visualise, identify the main idea and give an opinion.
- Use the text to clarify vocabulary.
- Use the text to introduce appropriate print conventions, phonological patterns and visual information.
- The student whose news has been recorded illustrates the text.

Example Year 1 (K)

Sam has new shoes. They are awesome! He can run very fast in his shoes.

Questions:
What has Sam got?
Why do you think Sam has new shoes?
Why do you think he can run very fast in his shoes?
Do you think it is good that Sam has new shoes? Why do you think that?

Vocabulary: What does *awesome* mean? What other words might mean the same?

Print Conventions: exclamation mark, full stop, capital letters (**Sam**, **They**, **He**).

Visual Information: bold text.

Phonological Pattern: digraph *sh- shoes*.

Phonological Pattern: word family *-an*.

Connections: How did you feel when you got new shoes?

Summarise: What is this news item mainly about (one sentence)?

LINKING THE LANGUAGE STRANDS | NEW REVISED EDITION

Following Years at School
- Summarise the previous day's article.
- Introduce the new article, asking the students to think critically about the text and predict its content, using headings, captions, labels, pictures or any other visual information.
- Read the text together, practising processing strategies to solve any unknown words.
- Use the text to clarify vocabulary.
- Use comprehension strategies — ask questions (literal and higher order), ask the students to visualise, identify the main idea, evaluate and give an opinion.
- Use the text to introduce or reinforce appropriate print conventions, phonological patterns and visual information.

Example Year 4 (G3)

> Picture from a newspaper or magazine.
>
> A pod of whales was stranded on Piper Beach. Many people volunteered to help the whales back into the water. It was a difficult task as the whales were extremely large and heavy.
>
> Volunteers worked throughout the night. By dawn, most of the whales were free.

Questions:
Why was it a difficult task to move the whales?
How do you think the whales came to be stranded?
Why do you think the volunteers had to work throughout the night?
Do you think the volunteers should have worked throughout the night? Why do you think that?

Vocabulary: clarify the words *pod* and *volunteered*.

Print Conventions: capitals for names (*Piper Beach*).

Visual Information: caption.

Phonological Pattern: suffix *-ly extremely*.

Summarise: What is this news article mainly about (key point/s)?

Visualise: What picture were you getting in your head when you read this article?

Shared Reading Using a News and Views Book

Suggested Format

Prepare a large book made from blank paper. Select an article that is appropriate to the interest level and developmental stage of the students. The news article needs to include a heading, a picture and text.

The teacher summarises the article in language that encourages the students to give an opinion or comment.

Grouping: Whole class.

Time Slot: At the beginning of the day.

Duration: 10 minutes Friday.

- Look at the visual information on the article and discuss this, e.g., heading, picture.
- Ask the students to predict what the article could be about.
- Read the article together, clarifying the vocabulary.
- Encourage discussion by asking the students to respond with an opinion or question or comment about the article.
- Below the summarised article, the teacher records one opinion, or "view", in a different coloured pen.

Example

DOG HAS NINETEEN PUPPIES

Picture and short caption from a newspaper or magazine.

This mother dog had nineteen puppies. Harley helps the mother to look after them. It is very hard work.

View: Ana
It is a good thing that Harley is helping the mother.

Clarify what is meant by *hard work*.

SPIDER FOUND

Picture and article from a newspaper or magazine.

A deadly black widow spider was found in a shipping container that had come from San Francisco. Inspectors from the Ministry of Agriculture and Forestry were called in to fumigate the container.

View: Waitori
I am glad the containers were fumigated because we don't want black widows in New Zealand.

Clarify the word *fumigate*.

2. Guided Reading

A guided reading approach is used for small groups or individual students. The students are grouped together according to their needs or levels. The purpose of the guided reading lesson is to guide students through the text, helping them to:

- develop an understanding of what is involved in reading
- develop their comprehension and critical responses to the text
- learn, practise and integrate their processing strategies (it is very important that beginning readers are shown how to make use of graphophonic information to identify words that are causing difficulty)
- build confidence.

The groupings must be viewed as flexible and the students need to be monitored by means of observation and running records.

Time Allocation: 10–20 minutes, depending on stage.

Note: There is no set formula for guided reading and the approach can vary according to the stage of the student and the individual text. The following are suggested approaches only.

Emergent Stage (1)

Focus – Vocabulary (Word Bank Building), Thinking Critically

Use texts that focus on building a high-frequency word bank. It is important that students be able to recognise a bank of known words automatically.

At this stage, the bank of high-frequency words could be:

I	am	a	here	is	this	look
we	went	like	can	me	and	said
come	for	he	my	to	the	

Working Through a Text – Suggested Format (Emergent Stage 1)

Before Reading the Text

- Focus the students' attention on the front cover. Introduce words — front, back, cover, title — if not known. Talk briefly about what the students can see. Read the title.

- Work spread by spread through the text. Talk about the illustrations and initiate discussion. Stop where appropriate and ask a question the students can discuss with a partner. Read the text *to* the students.

Reading the Text

- Return to the first page. Focus the students' attention on the text, talking about the starting point. Ask the students to read the text, pointing to the words. Ensure that the students establish one-to-one correspondence.

After Reading the Text

- Ask the students to retell orally what happened in the story.
- Ask the students literal and higher order questions, e.g., *Why do you think … ?, What do you think … ?, What might happen if … ?, How do you know …? Do you think … ? Why?*
- Give the students an opportunity to relate the message of the story to their own experiences, making a text to self connection.
- Focus the students' attention on any visual information in the text and discuss, e.g., bold text, increasing type size, illustrative text.
- Using the text, get the students to identify a high-frequency word that is focused on in the text. Ask questions that encourage the students to look at the spelling patterns and letter/sound relationships within the word. Ask the students to use individual whiteboards, if available, to practise writing the word.
- Focus on one initial consonant. Get the students to circle the letter with their fingers. Ask the students to write the letter on their whiteboards.
- Get the students to read the book to themselves and observe their reading behaviour.
- If appropriate, use an idea in the text to stimulate a visual or written response that can be collated into a booklet for independent reading. (It is suggested that one group per day processes information this way.)

Emergent Stage (2) – Fiction Text

Before Reading the Text

- Focus the students' attention on the front cover and either tell them what the story is about or ask them to predict. (Make this brief.)
- Read the title.
- "Walk" through the book, focusing the students' attention on the illustrations and initiating discussion.
- Where appropriate, predict what might happen next.
- At some time during this "walk", allow the students time to discuss and question with a partner.

Reading the Text

- Get the students to focus on the text.
- Read it together. (The text should be repetitive, so that once the pattern is established the students will be able to do this confidently.)
- Focus on and discuss any vocabulary that occurs in the reading. Ensure that the students know the meaning of any words.
- Observe the students, noting whether they have established one-to-one correspondence.

After Reading the Text

- Ask the students to retell orally what happened in the story.
- Ask the students literal and higher order questions, e.g., *What do you think … ?, Why do you think … ?, What might happen if … ?, How do you know … ?*
- Discuss the problem and how it was solved.
- Talk about the characters and share something about them.
- Discuss the setting of the story.
- Encourage the students to relate the story to their own experiences, making a text to self connection.

- Use the text to explore language. Ask questions that encourage the students to focus on the spelling patterns and letter/sound relationships within words. Introduce or reinforce vocabulary, print conventions, phonological patterns and visual information. One spread is often sufficient. Say, *Make a circle with your finger around the letter* b, *a word, a sentence, a full stop, a capital letter, a word that is bold, a word that belongs to the word family* at.
Reinforce, using individual whiteboards.
- Allow the students time to read the story independently, observing their reading behaviour.
- Use an idea in the text to stimulate a visual or written response that can be collated into a booklet for further independent reading. (It is suggested that only one group per day processes information this way.)

The book now becomes part of each student's independent reading resource and is used for independent practice daily.

Emergent Stage (2) – Non-fiction Text

Before Reading the Text

- Focus the students' attention on the front cover and either tell them what the book is about or ask them to predict.
- Read the title. If appropriate, ask the students what they know about the subject of the book.
- Focus the students' attention on the index and talk about what they are going to find out in the book.
- "Walk" through the book, focusing on the photographs, captions, labels and illustrations. Talk about the information they are providing, initiating discussion.
- At some time during this "walk", ask a question the students can discuss with a partner.

Reading the Text

- Get the students to focus on the text.
- Read the text together, noting whether the students have established one-to-one correspondence.
- Focus on and discuss any vocabulary that occurs during the reading. Ensure that the students know the meaning of any words.

After Reading the Text

- Ask the students what they have learned from reading the book.
- Give them an opportunity to recall some information or share something they have learned with a partner.
- Ask the students literal and higher order questions, e.g., *What … ?, Why … ?, How … ?*
- Encourage the students to make a text to self connection with the topic or ideas in the book.
- Use the text to ask the students questions that focus on the spelling patterns and letter/sound relationships within words.
- Focus on print conventions, phonological patterns (phonic knowledge and phonemes) and visual information (as with fiction text).
- Allow the students time to read the book independently, observing their reading behaviour.
- Use an idea in the text to stimulate a visual or written response that can be collated into a booklet for further independent reading. (It is suggested that only one group per day processes information in this way.)

The book now becomes part of each student's independent reading resource and is used for independent practice daily.

Early Stage (1) – Fiction Text

Before Reading the Text
- Introduce the story. Focus the students' attention on the cover illustration.
- Get the students to use the title and illustrations to predict, e.g., *What do you think this story could be about?*
- Use the terminology *title, author, illustrator* and *illustrations*.
- Go through some of the book, focusing the students' attention on the illustrations and asking higher order questions, e.g., *How do you think ... ?, Why do you think ... ?, What do you think ... ?*
- Where appropriate, ask the students a question they can discuss with a partner.

Reading the Text
- Ask the students to read the story. Ensure that they look carefully at the text. If they don't know a word, get the students to practise the processing strategies that are appropriate. These could be:
  - attending and searching the text for familiar text features, syntactical patterns and information in pictures
  - predicting what the word might be by drawing on prior knowledge and experience of language
  - cross-checking and confirming that the word makes sense and fits with the information already processed
  - detecting that an error has been made and searching for additional information to get the right meaning (self-correcting).
- Discuss any new vocabulary as it occurs in the reading. Ensure that the students know the meaning of any new words.

After Reading the Text
- Ask the students to retell the story.
- Talk about the word *plot* and discuss.
- Ask the students to recall the characters and say something about them.
- Discuss where the story took place (setting).
- Encourage the students to think about the message or theme of the story.
- Encourage the students to ask questions about the story.
- Encourage the students to relate the story to their own experiences, making text to self connections.
- On one spread only, use the text to introduce, reinforce or examine: print conventions, phonological patterns (phonic knowledge and phonemes) and visual information.
  e.g., Say, *Make a circle with your finger around a word that means ... ; around a blend, a digraph, quotation marks, a question mark, an exclamation mark, a word family*.
- Allow the students time to read the story independently, observing their reading behaviour.
- Get the students to read some of the story together, practising fluency (flow and phrasing).
- Use an idea in the text to stimulate a written or visual response to the story, if desired.

The book now becomes part of each student's independent reading resource and is used for independent practice.

Early Stage (1) – Non-fiction Text

Before Reading the Text

- Focus the students' attention on the title, author and photographs. Ask the students what they think they might find out in this book.
- Ask the students what they know about the topic.
- Focus the students' attention on the index. Ask them questions such as, *What page/s would we look on if we wanted to find out about ... ?*
- Look at the photographs over a two or three-page sequence and ask the students questions related to them (critical thinking).

Reading the Text

- Ask the students to read the text. If a word is not known, practise the processing strategies (as with fiction text).
- Discuss any new vocabulary as it occurs in the reading. Ensure that the students know the meaning of any new words.

After Reading the Text

- At the end of the text, ask the students what new information they have found out.
- Ask literal and higher order questions about the information.
- Ask the students to discuss some questions with a partner.
- Encourage the students to make a text to self connection with the topic or ideas in the book.
- On one or two spreads (as with fiction text), introduce, reinforce or examine: print conventions, phonological patterns (phonic knowledge and phonemes) and visual information.
- Allow the students time to read the book independently, observing their reading behaviour.
- Use an idea from the text to stimulate a written or visual response to the book.

The book now becomes part of each student's independent reading resource and is used for independent practice.

Early Stage (2) – Fiction Text

Introducing Guided Silent Reading

Before Reading the Text
- Introduce the story. Focus the students' attention on the cover illustration.
- Get the students to form a hypothesis about the text, e.g., *What do you think this story could be about?*
- Use the terminology *title, author, illustrator* and *illustration*.

Reading the text
- Focus on the illustrations on the first two spreads.
- Ask questions to initiate discussion.
- Pose a literal question that will be answered after the reading, e.g., *Why did … ? Why do … ?, How do you know … ? Was … ?* Then ask the students to read the text on the first two spreads with their eyes.
- Get the students to find the answer to the literal question on the page and read it aloud.
- Clarify any vocabulary the students may have had difficulties with. Ensure that processing strategies (see Early Stage 1, Fiction, *Reading the Text*) are being reinforced.
- Ask the students literal and higher order questions.
- Look at the next two spreads. Get the students to read aloud, practising flow and phrasing (fluency).
- Alternate reading silently and aloud together throughout the remaining text, attending to print conventions and visual information.
- Encourage the students to ask questions and discuss them with a partner.

After Reading the Text
- Discuss and think critically about plot, characters and settings.
- Encourage the students to make text to self connections with the message in the text.
- Use the text to introduce, reinforce or examine: print conventions, phonological patterns (phonic knowledge and phonemes) and visual information on one spread of text only (as with Early Stage 1, Fiction, *After Reading*).
- Allow the students time to read the story independently.
- Encourage the students to respond to the story, if desired, using written or visual language. Collate the responses into a book for further independent reading.

Student responses to guided reading texts can be collated into books for independent reading.

Examples

> **By the end of the Early stage, students should be able to:**
> - understand the purpose of a text
> - understand the literal message of a text
> - make text to self connections with the message of a text
> - answer literal and inferential questions orally
> - ask questions related to a text
> - use reading strategies (processing and comprehension) to decode words, construct meaning and think critically
> - know all letter names and sounds
> - know all blends and digraphs
> - have a level of phonemic awareness (hear sounds in words)
> - have a bank of high-frequency words they can recognise automatically (about 200)
> - know and use in their reading the following print conventions:
>
>   **full stop**
>
>   **comma**
>
>   **speech marks**
>
>   **exclamation mark**
>
>   **question mark**
> - read with flow and phrasing
> - interpret some visual information:
>
>   **bold font, labels, captions, illustrative text, lists, illustrations, photographs, index, symbols, simple maps, trails, mapping charts, signs, speech bubbles, thought bubbles, simple graphs, flow diagrams**
> - read *selected* unseen texts independently.

Fluency Stage (1)

At the Fluency stage of guided reading, students should be introduced to a variety of text forms. The approach to guided reading at this stage depends on the text form. Some text forms, e.g., narrative, can be completed in one guided reading session. Other text forms, e.g., advertisements or explanations, may be taken over several guided reading sessions.

Text Form — Narrative

Before Reading the Text
- Introduce the book. Discuss the title, author and cover illustration briefly.
- Examine some illustrations and discuss what the story could be about and what type of text form it could be. Ask the students to form hypotheses.
- Establish the purpose of the reading.

Reading the Text
- Give the students a response sheet (see page 45) and allow the students time to read the story independently, using the response sheet to note words or phrases they need to clarify and to formulate a question for discussion. Encourage the students to ask a variety of questions — literal and higher order (inference, evaluation and reaction).

After Reading the Text
- Bring the students together for a discussion.
- Discuss the students' questions and vocabulary on their sheets. Establish some reasons why the story is fiction.
- Look at the student targets (see page 26) and select those that can be focused on using this text.
- Discuss the characteristics of a narrative. Talk about the plot, the problem — if any — it raises and the solution.
- Discuss the characters, setting and theme and get the students to think critically about them. Encourage the students to make text to self, text to text and text to world connections.
- Summarise the main ideas related to the storyline.
- Use the text to introduce, reinforce or examine: vocabulary, print conventions, phonological patterns and visual information.
- Encourage the students to respond to the text, if appropriate, in a written or visual way. Collate the students' responses into a booklet for further independent reading.
- The text can be returned to on another day with the purpose of examining how it is written — "The craft of the writer".

Other Text Forms — e.g., Recount, Manual, Diary, Report, Advertisement, Brochure, Interview, Menu, Lists, Directions, Descriptions

Before the Reading the Text
- Introduce the book. Discuss the title, author and cover illustration briefly.
- Ask the students what they think this text could be about. Encourage them to form hypotheses.
- Ask what type of text this could be and who it might be written for.
- Establish the purpose of the reading.

Reading the Text
- Give the students a response sheet (see page 45) and allow the students time to read the book independently, using the response sheet for questions and vocabulary.

After Reading the Text
- Bring the students together for a discussion. Discuss the students' questions and vocabulary.
- Encourage the students to make text to self, text to text and text to world connections where appropriate.
- Look at the student targets (see page 26) and select those that can be focused on using this text.
- Discuss with the students the way the text has been written. Compare the text with other text forms.
- Use the text to introduce, reinforce or examine: vocabulary, print conventions, phonological patterns and visual information.
- Select an idea in the text to stimulate a written or visual response to the book that can be collated into a booklet for further independent reading.
- The text can be returned to on another day with the purpose of examining how it is written — "The craft of the writer".

Example of a Response Sheet

Title:
Text Form:
I need to clarify (word/s):   My Guess   Dictionary meaning   Other word/s that mean the same (synonyms)
A question:

Text Form — Informational Explanation, Informational Report

These texts are not usually completed in one guided reading session.
The text can be returned to over a period of days, using a specific focus.

Before Reading the Text

- Focus the students' attention on the title, author and photographs.
- Ask the students what they think the book is about and form hypotheses.
- Get the students to visualise the text content.
- Ask the students what they know about the subject.
- Make a list of what they know about the subject or get the students to sketch their current understanding of the topic.
- Focus on the index and the table of contents. Ask the students, *If you want to find out about … where would you look?*
- Discuss with the students how to retrieve information and what to use to do it.
- Select a specific topic within the text, e.g., text subject — elephants; specific topic — trunks. Locate the pages that refer to the topic by using the index or contents page. Get the students to check by locating the pages referred to.

Reading the Text

- Get the students to read the pages relating to the specific topic silently.
- On completion of the reading, clarify any vocabulary.
- Encourage the students to ask questions orally about what they have read, to clarify their understanding of the topic and promote discussion.
- Get the students to summarise orally the text pages they have read.

After Reading the Text

- Use the pages read to introduce, reinforce or examine print conventions, phonological patterns and visual information.
- Ask the students what they have learned about the topic covered in the text, making text to self, text to text and text to world connections. Repeat over several days if necessary.

Final Reading

- Once the entire text has been read, ask the students what they now know about the subject. Refer to the initial list or sketches and add the new information.
- Discuss with the students the way the text has been written and compare it with other text forms.

Using the Information (if appropriate)

- The students can use the information in different ways, depending on the text, e.g., they could:
  - look at other books or a website dealing with a similar topic and compare the information offered
  - present the information they have learned to other students in the class.

Fluency Stage (2)

At this stage of reading, the guided reading component will need to extend the students' understanding of different text forms and their structures and features. It is suggested that the same text form be the focus over a block of time, so that a deep understanding of the characteristics and structure is established.

Text Form — Narrative

Follow a pattern similar to that suggested for the beginning of the Fluency stage, or examine the features of narrative texts by focusing on one feature at a time and developing an understanding of this. The following is an example of using several texts to examine the features of narrative writing.

Plots

Over several guided reading lessons, focus on the plots of the stories. Encourage the students to think critically about:

- where the idea for the story could have come from
- whether the story could actually have happened or not
- how the story developed, e.g., beginning, development, climax, resolution, ending.

Encourage the students to express an opinion on:

- how the illustrations or pictures have been used and whether they help the reader understand the plot
- which parts of the story were the most exciting, less clear, more interesting, slow, lively etc.

Discuss with the students any special features that contribute to the plot, e.g., chapter headings, link sentences.

Extend and enrich the students' vocabularies by introducing and exploring the following terms relating to plots:

> main events, situation, action, interaction, plot, sub-plot, introduction, climax, problem, crisis, solution, resolution, conclusion, chapter, paragraph, episode

Process information by:

- comparing the plot with the plots of stories the students have read
- looking at introductions and conclusions and comparing their effectiveness
- examining wordless books and creating text for them.

Characters

In a similar way, examine the characters in several stories. It is important that the students be encouraged to think critically about the characters, their actions, their development and their relationships and to think about how they feel about the characters in the light of their own concerns and actions.

Extend and enrich the students' vocabulary by introducing and exploring the following terms relating to characters:

> major/minor characters, hero/heroine, dialogue, conversation, facial features, values, actions, manner, appearance

The students could process information by describing the characters from a story in various ways, e.g., through role-play, designing a poster or making a picture.

Setting

Examine the settings in narrative stories. Encourage the students to think critically about how the author has established the setting. Does the setting change? What mood is created when the setting changes? What would the plot be like in a different setting? How does the setting affect the characters?

Students will need to be aware of: the place, the time of day, the weather, the season, the atmosphere, the tone and mood of the story.

Extend and enrich the students' vocabulary by introducing and exploring the following terms relating to setting:

> dark, sombre, bright, cheerful, urban, rural
> plus words related to: seasons, shapes, sounds, textures, feelings and colours

Students could process information about themes by drawing a picture, map or sketch of the setting.

Theme

Examine themes in narrative stories. The students need to be encouraged to identify the themes in a number of different stories and compare them. Encourage the students to think critically about what the author could be trying to say through the story.

Extend and enrich the students' vocabulary by introducing and exploring the following terms relating to theme:

> injustice, snobbery, power, courage, fear, superficial, selfish, realistic, romantic, subject, message, beliefs, attitudes, issue

The students could process information by using the author's themes in their own writing.

Text Form – Report

Examining Reports and Thinking Critically

Ask the students what a report is.

Look at a report.

Ask the students how we know it is a report.

Refer to the chart showing the steps to follow when writing a report (writing section, page 75) and compare it with the characteristics and framework of the report being examined.

Exploring Language

Students need to be familiar with the following terminology:

> fact, opinion, evidence, objective, neutral, subjective, theory, proof, example, alternative, true, false, prejudice, bias, problem, solution, compare, contrast

Use this vocabulary in relation to the report, if appropriate.

Processing Information

Discuss other ways in which the report could have been presented.

The students could:

- present the report in an alternative way
- write a newspaper report, science report or weather report.

Text Form — Procedural

Examining Procedurals and Thinking Critically

Give the students a set of instructions (procedural). Ask them to read them and note the places in which they experienced difficulty. Suggest solutions.

Discuss the purpose of the procedural.

Exploring Language

Refer to the chart showing the steps to follow when writing procedurals (writing section, page 74) and compare it with the characteristics and framework of the procedural being examined.

Discuss the clarity of the sequence of actions described.

Discuss the layout of the text and whether it makes the instructions easier to understand.

Look at the vocabulary used for linking, e.g., first, next, last.

Exploring Language

The students need to be familiar with the following terminology:

> heading, title, subtitle, purpose, goal, sequence, step, stage, operating instructions

Use this vocabulary as it arises in examining procedurals.

Processing Information

The students can design their own set of instructions, e.g., for a game, a recipe etc.

Text Form — Advertisements

Examining Advertisements and Thinking Critically

Examine an advertisement and get the students to predict the targeted audience.

Discuss what the advertisement is trying to promote or sell and to whom.

Encourage the students to think about how the advertisement grabs attention.

Exploring Language

Refer to the chart showing the steps to follow when writing persuasive arguments (writing section, page 75) and decide what is applicable to the advertisement being examined.

Look for:

> emotive language, facts and opinions, simple structures, persuasive words and phrases, bias, abbreviated sentences, tense used, constant repetition

Thinking Critically and Exploring Language

Compare different advertisements for the same product. Compare the claims made by each advertisement.

Sort advertisements into categories according to:

- content
- effectiveness
- look
- tone
- pace
- urgency
- use of images.

Compare the text features. Look at the text shape, spellings, abbreviations, sentence lengths.

Exploring Language

Examine the language used in the advertisements, e.g., action words, positive words, colourful comparisons, abbreviated sentences, metaphor, imagery, slang.

Processing Information

The students could make up their own advertisements, using the examples they have gathered.

Other texts, such as recounts, descriptions and explanations, can be examined in a similar manner.

3. Independent Reading

Independent reading is a vital component of any reading programme. It allows the students to practise their reading competencies and to read at their own pace. It builds their vocabulary, helps comprehension and promotes fluency.

Emergent and Early Stage (1)

At this stage use:

- texts that have been introduced in guided reading
- group books generated from processing information during guided reading
- reading-related learning centres, e.g., shared books, poetry, news books, the library.

End of Early Stage (2)

At this stage use:

- unseen texts selected from a level below the student's instructional level
- texts that have been used for guided reading
- group books generated by processing information during guided reading
- reading-related learning centres.

Fluency Stage (1)

Materials:

- Boxes of selected reading material, e.g., one box of fiction, one box of non-fiction. Include short and longer texts and identify them with a label.
- A variety of response sheets for plot, characters, setting, non-fiction.
- A scrapbook for each student to paste in responses to texts.

Examples of Response Sheets

Plot Sheets

Plot	Plot	Plot	Plot
Title: Author: You can make a sequence chart like this. 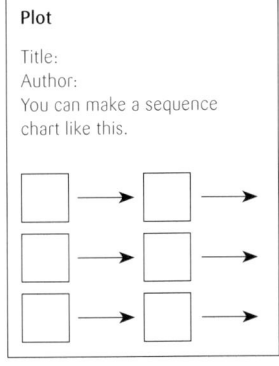	Title: Look at three books you have read. What is the problem? What is the solution? | Problem | Solution | |---|---| | Problem | Solution | | Problem | Solution |	Title: Author: You can make a flow diagram.	Title: Author: Think about the story. Make a comic strip with the same ideas.

Character Sheets

Characters	Characters	Characters	Characters
Title: Author: You can write a letter to one of the characters in the book. Character:	Title: Author: You can compare two characters in the book. Make a list of words that describe them. | Character 1 | Character 2 |	Title: Author: You can draw a character or characters and write words that tell something about them.	Title: Author: You can make a list of all the characters in the story.

Setting Sheets

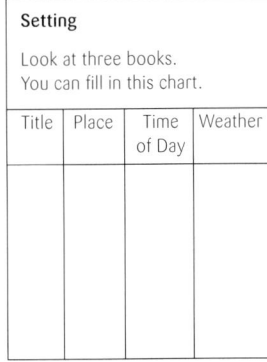

Setting	Setting	Setting
Title: Author: You can draw where the story took place. Add some words that tell what the place was like.	Title: Author: You can think of some other places where the story could have taken place. Draw and label. You can think of places where the story could not have taken place. Draw and give a reason.	Title: Author: Describe a setting at the beginning of the story. Describe a setting at the end of the story.

Non-fiction Sheets

Non-fiction
Title:
Author:
Topic:
You can make a web.

—— TOPIC ——

Non-fiction
Title:
Author:
Topic:
What questions do you have?

You can ask an expert, find another book, look on the Internet.

Non-fiction
Title:
Author:
Topic:
What did you learn?

Draw and label.

Non-fiction
Title:
Author:
Topic:
What other books can you find on the same topic?
You can make a list.

Reading Record Sheet

The student fills in the book that he/she processed using response sheets.

My Reading Record				
Date	Title	Author	Fiction	Non-fiction

Instruction Card

Prepare an instruction card so that the students know what to do at independent reading time.

What to Do
1) Read six shorter books or one long book.
2) Choose one book and write its details on your reading record sheet.
3) Choose one activity to do from the response sheets.
4) Paste your activity into your scrapbook.
5) Go to a learning centre or continue reading.

Fluency Stage (2)

The independent reading programme for students at this stage could be established as follows:

- Set up a display in the classroom of material students can choose from, e.g., a variety of books, both fiction and non-fiction, chapter books and picture books; other reading material, including magazines, atlas, thesaurus, brochures, newspapers.
- Provide a personal reading record book (see page 56).
- Establish routines.

Suggested Independent Reading Routine

- Select the material/book you want to read.
- Read your chosen material/book.
- When you have finished reading, put your name on the conference chart (see below).
- Fill in your personal reading record.
- Choose an activity or read a new book.
- When the activity is complete, put your name on the sharing timetable.
- Share the material/book you read and your response with the class or group.

Note: Not everything read needs to have a response. Set a time limit for the response. Once every two weeks is probably sufficient for a conference. Once every three weeks for a response.

Example of a Conference Chart

	Mon	Tues	Wed	Thurs	Fri
Tom	●	●	●	●	●
Sue	●	●	●	●	●
Sally	●	●	●	●	●

Example of a Sharing Timetable

	Mon	Tues	Wed	Thurs	Fri
Bob	●	●	●	●	●
Mark	●	●	●	●	●
Lee	●	●	●	●	●

Example of Personal Reading Record Book

Suggested Activities to Follow the Reading

The following are examples of activities that could follow the independent reading.

Story Map	Prepare a story map. Label the main features. Explain your ideas.
Time Line	Place the story on a line. Think about the time and distance between events.
Flow Chart	Select the main points of the story. Make a flow chart to show ideas.
Diary	Make up a diary entry for a character. Make entries for the day before and the day after the event.
Letters	Write letters between two of the story's characters. Write a letter to someone outside the story. Write a letter to the author.
Newspaper	Write a newspaper report based on an idea from the story or article. Write an advertisement related to the characters in the story. Write a newspaper article. Write a letter to the editor.
Semantic Web	Choose a character from the story. Put the name or drawing of the character in the middle of the page. Fill in as many details about the character as you can around the circle. If you have read a non-fiction book or article, you can do a factual semantic web.
Become a Storyteller	Use an idea in the text to tell the story the best way you can.
Comparison Chart	Make a comparison chart to show the differences and/or similarities between two characters in two different stories.
Facts/Opinions	Make a chart to show facts and opinions from the story or article.
Cause and Effect	Make a diagram that shows an action in the book or article and the reaction that it caused.
Present	Present the story or article, or part of it, using an overhead projector, tape recorder or video.
Family Tree	Make a family tree of the characters in the story.
Map	Draw a map to show where the story or article took place.
Design/Model	Make a design or model from an idea in the book or article.

Individual Reading Goals

It is important for the students to establish their own reading goals and assess themselves against these goals.

> *A Self-Assessment Reference Chart*
>
> What is the purpose for reading?
>
> What have I learned to do?
>
> What am I learning to do?
>
> What did I learn from what I read?
>
> What do I need help with?
>
> What do I do when I need help?
>
> What goals can I set?

Conferencing

Conferences are discussions between the student and the teacher. They are used so that:

- the student can share successes
- the teacher can diagnose difficulties
- the teacher can assess the skills and reading interests of a student
- the student can discuss styles of writing and features of the text
- the student can compare texts
- the teacher can assist students to:
  - select material to read
  - focus on what they are trying to learn
  - understand unfamiliar words
  - summarise the text
  - focus on the language features of texts
  - locate and use information from texts
  - set goals for themselves.

The students can establish their own reading conference chart to fill in after the conference with the teacher.

Example of a Reading Conference Chart for Student to Fill in
(Make it a full-sized page.)

Conference Chart	Name:
I can:	Goals

Reciprocal Reading

Reciprocal reading is a method of small group instruction, usually undertaken with students who are at the Fluency stage of reading.

Students must be able to work well independently. Reciprocal reading works best with non-fiction material.

A group of students is formed. The teacher begins by taking the role of leader to establish the pattern, but later hands the role over to the students and becomes a group member or withdraws, when appropriate.

Suggested Format

The group works through the text, according to the following pattern:

- *Predicting* — the leader predicts what will come next in the text, based on prior knowledge or visual information. The students read an assigned piece of the text.
- *Clarifying* — the leader deals with difficulties in the text, e.g., vocabulary, structure, new concepts. After recognising the problem, the readers can establish the meaning in different ways, e.g., by rereading, using the context of the passage or using reference material (atlas, encyclopedia, road map).
- *Question Generating* — the readers pose questions and answer themselves.
- *Summarising* — the leader identifies the key points in the text.
- The pattern is repeated with a new leader, who assigns the next portion of the text to be read.

4. Reading to Students

Reading to students is the single most important activity for building the knowledge required for eventual success in learning to read. This must be done daily and is appropriate for all students, including those who are accurate, fluent readers.

It is important to choose the books to be read carefully. Students need to be read good literature, rich in language, imagery and other literary devices. Reading aloud to students needs to be expressive and provide a good model, so that students will recognise books as a source of pleasure.

Teacher Targets

- To create and nurture a love of reading.
- To enrich and extend vocabulary.
- To develop awareness of the sound of language.
- To encourage students to respond to language and meaning in text by engaging them in conversations about the text and helping them to make connections.

Sharing Time

At the conclusion of the reading block, it is important to allow time for students to share. This is a valuable way to promote interest in material the students might not have read themselves.

Students at the end of the Early stage or the beginning of the Fluency stage may share something they have done in an independent reading centre, or a book they have read independently.

Students at the advanced stage of Fluency, whose names are on the sharing timetable, will share the independent activity that followed their reading.

Reading Block Agendas

Agenda 1

A suggested schedule to use with students reading at the Emergent to Fluency stage (1).

Monday to Thursday
A) Shared reading (10 minutes)
B) Guided reading/Independent reading (45 minutes)

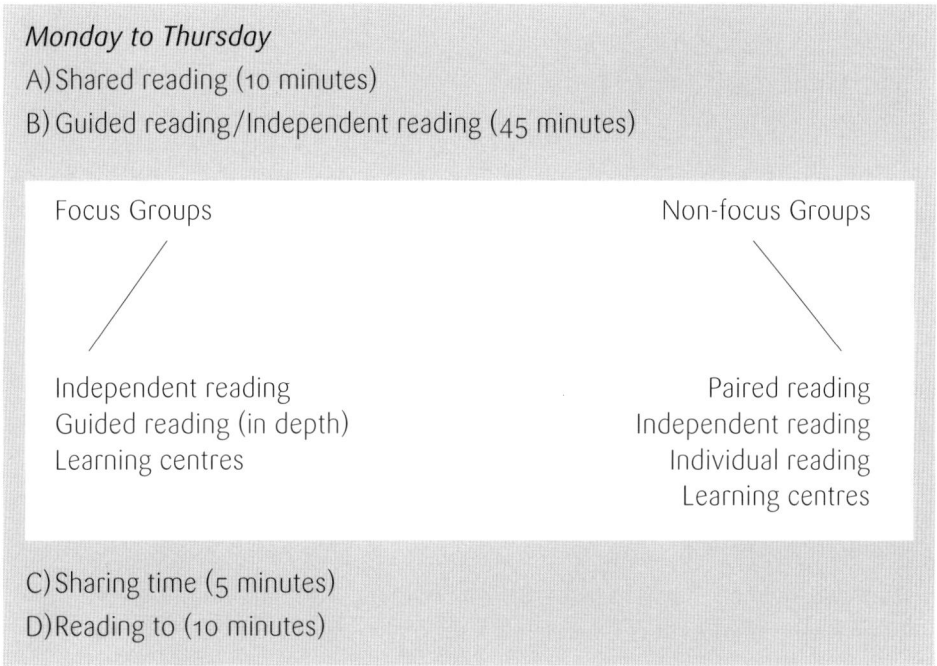

C) Sharing time (5 minutes)
D) Reading to (10 minutes)

Guided Reading

The groups selected that day to do an in-depth guided reading lesson are the focus groups. It is very difficult to give quality time to all reading groups every day. Therefore, it is suggested that two groups a day might be the focus groups.

Paired Reading

Students in the non-focus groups can share a book with a partner in their own group or another non-focus group.

Individual Reading

It is important that the teacher allows time to hear some students read individually each day on a rotating basis.

Processing Information

Choose one group per day from the focus groups (Monday–Thursday). Provide them with a meaningful activity that can be collated into a book for that group's independent reading.

Agenda 2

A suggested schedule to use with students reading at the Fluency stage (2).

Monday to Thursday
  A) Shared reading (10 minutes)
  B) Paired reading (45 minutes)
  C) Independent reading (45 minutes)
  D) Guided reading or reciprocal reading (45 minutes)
      Conferencing — all children conferenced over a two-week span
  E) Sharing time (5 minutes)
  F) Reading to (10 minutes)

Guided Reading

Students at this stage may only require one or two guided reading sessions per week. This will depend on the class size and needs of the students.

Reciprocal Reading

This may only be included as part of the reading programme once every two weeks, or when it is considered beneficial.

OVERVIEW OF THE WRITING PROGRAMME

Teacher Targets	Methods
To establish a balanced writing programme.	By allocating time for writing with, writing for and writing by the student.
To create a love of writing.	By showing enthusiasm and making positive responses to the writer's message.
To encourage students to write regularly to record personal experiences.	By exposing students to examples of expressive writing.
To encourage students to write descriptively on a variety of topics, learning to shape ideas and experiment with language and form.	By exposing students to examples of poetic writing.
To encourage students to write instructions and recount events in authentic contexts.	By exposing students to examples of transactional writing.
To develop and extend students' vocabulary.	By reading and writing and oral interaction.
To accept students' approximations in initial drafts.	By focusing on what the student can do.
To recognise and cater for individual needs and differences.	By regular monitoring of writing, conferences and individual goal setting.
To give students time to write.	By having a timetable that allows students time to write independently.

Student Targets
These are the specific achievement objectives.
Emergent Stage (Level 1 i)
Surface Features – Tools
To have correct directional movement.
To leave spaces between words.
To use approximations.
To use approximations according to the sound heard at the beginning of words.
To begin to use some high-frequency words.
Deeper Features – Working with Message
To be able to choose a topic to write on.
To use their own experiences for writing.
To begin to talk about some features of their own writing.
To be able to present a piece of writing for others to share.
Process
To use illustrations to support meaning.
Approximate Age Band 4–5 years

Example of Writing, Emergent Stage (Level 1 i)

Student Targets

These are the specific achievement objectives.

Early Stage (Level 1 *ii/iii*)

Surface Features – Tools

To use beginning and end sounds of words.

To spell many high-frequency words correctly.

To use more correctly spelled words than approximations.

To begin to use some common spelling patterns.

To begin to understand and use capital letters and full stops.

To write sentences that make sense.

Deeper Features – Working with Message

To begin to gain audience interest.

To be able to choose an appropriate title.

To begin to understand the different purposes for writing and select from a wider range of topics and text forms.

To make an attempt to express personal experiences, explain, describe or give an opinion.

To use simple sentences with some variation in beginnings.

To begin to sequence ideas.

To begin to use simple conjunctions to join ideas.

To begin to use some compound sentences.

Process

To show simple planning.

To begin using editing skills:

- to place full stops
- to place capital letters
- to locate approximations by underlining
- to begin to correct approximations by using word sources.

To begin to realise that writing can involve a number of stages.

To begin to record and present information in different ways.

Approximate Age Band 6-7 years

Example Early Stage (Level 1 ii)

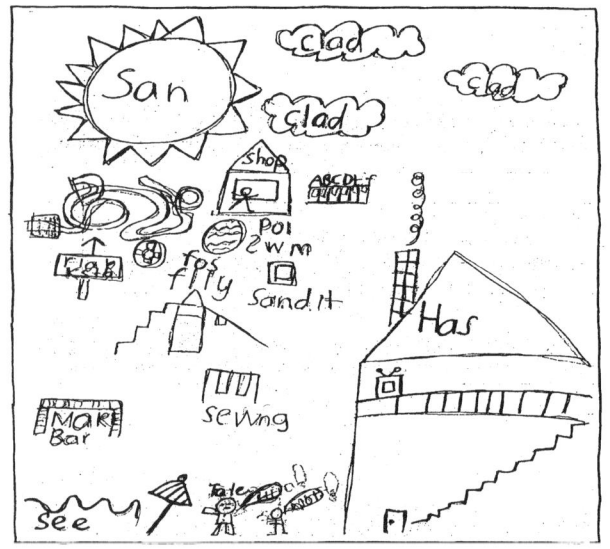

Fale

I like pues be kaas
They. are. chaube I
had a pue but It ran
a way wen I had It
I nos tow plya wfe
it

I like puppies because
they are chubby. I had
a puppy but it ran away.
When I had it I used to
play with it.

Example Early Stage (Level 1 iii)

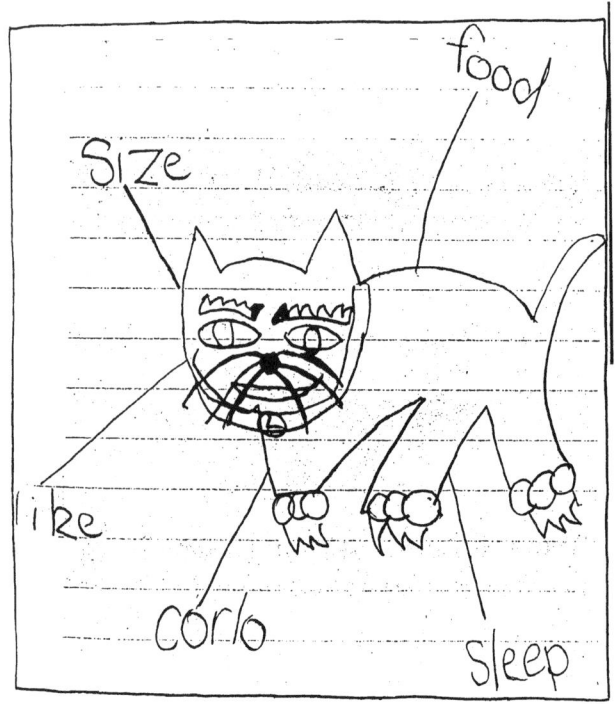

My Cat is ~~greay~~ grey
and ~~wite~~ white. He sleeps
~~undre~~ under my house.

He likes to eat

milk and bread

for ~~brekfast~~ breakfast. His size

is big. He likes to

~~walke~~ walk with me.

Example Fluency Stage (Level 2)

Example Fluency Stage (Level 3)

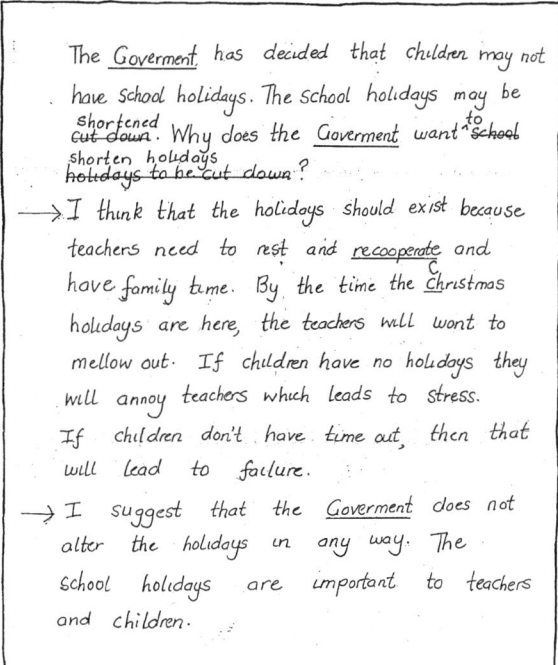

Student Targets

These are the specific achievement objectives.

Fluency Stage (Level 2)

Surface Features – Tools

To show a knowledge of consonant and vowel sounds, blends and common spelling patterns.

To be able to spell most high-frequency words correctly.

To use capital letters, full stops, commas, question marks and speech marks with some consistency.

To use most grammatical conventions: consistent tense, correctly formed sentences, correct prepositions.

Deeper Features – Working with Message

To understand the purpose of the writing.

To be able to recognise that different audiences and purposes require different language features.

To be able to write about personal experiences, explain, describe and give an opinion with some clarity.

To begin to show an awareness of audience by use of content and language choices.

To begin to use literary devices to enhance writing, where appropriate, e.g., similes, metaphors, analogies.

To be able to sequence with some confidence.

To be able to attempt more complex sentences.

To be able to vary sentence beginnings and length.

To be able to use a more comprehensive topic-related vocabulary.

To be able to experiment with vocabulary to achieve an intended effect.

Process

To be able to comment on their own or others' writing.

To be able to plan writing, if appropriate.

To use editing skills to:
- clarify the message of the writing
- add and delete to improve the message
- correct punctuation and spelling.

To be able to use a variety of resources to locate words or clarify unknown words.

Approximate Age Band 8-9 years

Student Targets
These are the specific achievement objectives.
Fluency Stage (Level 3)
Surface Features – Tools
To be able to demonstrate a good understanding of all basic sounds and patterns in written English.
To be able to spell all high-frequency words correctly.
To be able to punctuate correctly: capital letters, full stops, commas, question marks and speech marks, apostrophes, exclamation marks, colons, semi-colons, ellipses.
To use most grammatical conventions: consistent tense, correctly formed sentences, correct prepositions.
Deeper Features – Working with Message
To use a variety of means to gain audience interest, e.g., humour, choice of language.
To be able to write in a variety of ways.
To be able to record thoughts, feelings and ideas clearly.
To be able to use a language and writing style that is appropriate to the audience.
To be able to demonstrate a deliberate choice of appropriate language features and literary devices to enhance writing.
To convey personal views, feelings and experiences with sincerity.
To be able to shape ideas for effect.
To be able to organise ideas into paragraphs.
To be able to use a variety of sentence beginnings and lengths.
To use a wide range of vocabulary: adjectives, verbs etc.
Process
To be able to write independently for a sustained period of time.
To be able to respond to and appreciate their own and others' work.
To be able to use and respond confidently to feedback.
To be able to talk about the language features used.
To be able to plan writing carefully.
To be able to use a dictionary, thesaurus or other word sources confidently.
To be able to revise and edit their own work with confidence, adding, deleting and attending to punctuation and spelling.
Approximate Age Band 10+ years

ORGANISATION AND MANAGEMENT OF THE WRITING PROGRAMME

In a balanced writing programme, students need to meet with many different writing experiences. When considering the organisation and management of the written language programme, it is important to provide students with experiences in:

1. Writing with students
2. Writing for students
3. Writing by students

1. Writing with Students

Writing with students, or shared writing, is when the teacher and the students work together as a class or group to construct a piece of writing. The teacher is the scribe and explains and models the writing strategies appropriate to the stage and interest level of the class or group. The students contribute their ideas to the construction of the text. This should be a creative and enjoyable activity, but often a range of developmental stages are involved, so sessions need to be short and well paced.

Shared writing usually arises from a common experience, so that all the students can have some ownership of the writing.

Shared writing would be appropriate when:

- retelling a story that has been read to the class
- the class has been on a trip
- a visitor has been to school or to the classroom
- when an investigation or experiment has been carried out.

Interactive Writing

Interactive writing is similar to shared writing, but it involves all the students in scribing the common text. Each student has their own small whiteboard or paper and pen. The teacher still leads the construction of the writing, but the students write down the text themselves.

Depending on the writing stage, the teacher may need to model some words for the students to copy, but they are encouraged to attempt as much as they can by themselves.

Interactive writing works best with a small group of students and is particularly useful for students who come from non-English-speaking backgrounds.

2. Writing for Students

Writing for students is when the teacher takes control of the writing and demonstrates his or her own writing in front of the students, explaining each step of the construction.

Writing for students is usually done with a group of children at a similar developmental stage. Sessions should be short (10–15 minutes) and motivational.

Emergent Stage

Materials: whiteboard or large piece of blank paper, pens, alphabet cue card.

When writing for students at this stage:

- Have targets clearly in mind (see page 71).
- Tell the students what your writing is going to be about.
- Using simple graphics, show the students what will be in your writing.
- Verbalise the first sentence, showing students how a writer thinks in a "language chunk".
- Write the sentence in front of the students, using an alphabet card to demonstrate the link between letters and their sounds. Talk about direction and spaces. Focus on appropriate high-frequency words.
- Follow this pattern with two or three sentences.
- On completion of the writing, encourage the students to read the writing with you.
- Ask the students a literal and inferential question about your writing.
- Encourage the students to ask a question or make a comment about your writing.

Emergent Stage (1 i)

Surface Features – Tools
- direction
- spaces
- initial letters
- high-frequency words

Deeper Features – Working with Message
- topic
- using own experiences
- talking about writing
- illustrating published writing and sharing

Process
- simple planning
- illustrations and labels

Personal Experiences
Simple Descriptions

Early Stage (1 ii)

Surface Features – Tools
- beginning and end sounds
- high-frequency words
- spelling patterns
- capital letters/full stops

Deeper Features – Working with Message
- title
- audience
- purpose
- simple sentences
- sequencing ideas

Process
- planning
- editing: underlining errors

Personal Experiences
Simple Descriptions

Early Stage

When writing for students at this stage:
- Have targets clearly in mind.
- Say what the writing will be about.
- Use graphics to show the students what will be in your writing.
- Verbalise the first sentence, emphasising the position of the full stop.
- Write out the sentence, using an alphabet and blend card. Students can assist with this. Continue to focus on high-frequency words. Follow this pattern with the next three or four sentences.
- On completion of the writing, ask the students to read the writing with you.
- Encourage the students to make a comment on the message of your writing.
- Decide on a title for your writing.

Early Stage (1 iii)

Surface Features – Tools
- beginning and end sounds
- high-frequency words
- spelling patterns
- capital letters/full stops

Deeper Features – Working with Message
- title
- audience
- purpose
- simple sentences
- simple compound sentences (two or more main clauses joined)
- sequencing ideas

Process
- planning
- editing: underlining errors, correcting errors using dictionary, full stops/capital letters

Personal Experiences
Explanations
Simple Descriptions
Opinions

Fluency Stage (2)

Surface Features – Tools
- high-frequency words
- spelling patterns
- capital letters/full stops, commas, question marks, speech marks
- grammatical conventions: tenses, prepositions

Deeper Features – Working with Message
- title
- audience awareness: content, language, choices
- purpose
- varied sentence beginnings
- varied sentence length
- complex sentences
- extending vocabulary
- literary devices: simile, metaphor, analogy

Process
- planning
- editing: adding/deleting
  spelling
  underlining errors using a variety of word sources
  punctuation
- commenting on writing

Personal Experiences
Descriptions
Explanations
Opinions

Early and Fluency Stage

When writing for students at this stage:

- Have targets clearly in mind and which ones will be focused on.
- Explain to the students:
  - why you are writing (purpose)
  - who you are writing for (audience)
  - what you are going to write about (topic).
- Plan your writing in an appropriate way, according to the purpose, e.g., visual sequence, web if necessary.
- If a plan has been used, construct the writing in front of the students, referring to the plan and focusing on appropriate targets.
- Purposely omit some print conventions and make some spelling miscues in high-frequency words or words students can easily recognise as incorrect.
- Reread the writing, focusing on the message. Using a different coloured pen, demonstrate how to:
  - delete from the message
  - add to the message or insert.
- Reread the writing, focusing on punctuation. Use a different coloured pen to add punctuation omitted.
- Reread the writing, focusing on spelling miscues — underline these. Using a dictionary, demonstrate how to find the correct spelling and write this on the line above the miscue.
- Encourage the students to think critically about the writing, ask questions or make comments.
- Decide on a title for your writing.

Fluency Stage

Have targets clearly in mind and which ones will be focused on.

Fluency Stage (3)

Surface Features – Tools

- all basic sounds and patterns
- high-frequency words
- punctuation: capital letters/full stops, commas, question marks, speech marks, apostrophes, exclamation marks, colons, semi-colons, ellipses
- tenses, pronouns: *he, she, they* prepositions: *about, above, across, after, against, along, among, at, before, behind, below, beneath, beside, between, beyond, by, despite, during, except, for, from, in, inside* etc.

Deeper Features – Working with Message

- variety of ways of writing
- audience interest through humour, choice of words etc.
- language and writing style appropriate to the audience
- clarity of expression: thoughts, feelings
- personal feelings/views expressed with sincerity
- ideas shaped for effect
- variety of sentence beginnings and lengths
- wide range of vocabulary
- ideas organised into paragraphs
- literary devices: simile, metaphor, analogy

Process

- planning
- respond to writing
- respond to feedback
- talk about language features used
- revise and edit independently: adding/deleting, attending to punctuation and spelling

Text Forms at Fluency Stage

At this Fluency stage of writing, a greater focus needs to be placed on the structure and features of a variety of text forms. Teachers will need to demonstrate to the students the specific purpose of the writing and the framework around which this writing is developed. In order to do this, it is suggested that simple steps, to be followed when writing each text form, are clearly visible to the students as the writing is demonstrated. The following text form cards could be made.

Procedural — How to Find
1) Write the heading.
2) Write the steps in order.

Can you add a map, plan or diagrams to make your instructions clearer?

Procedural — How to Make
1) Write the heading.
2) Write a list of things that will be needed.
3) Write the steps in order.

Can you add diagrams to make the instructions clearer?

Procedural — How to Use
1) Write the heading.
2) Write the steps in order.

Can you add diagrams to make the instructions clearer?

Recount
1) Write an opening (*who, when, where, what*).
2) Write about events in order.
3) Write a conclusion.

Description
1) Think about what you are going to describe.
2) Make a list of descriptive words.
3) Write your description.

Is your description like a talking picture?

Explanation
1) Choose a topic.
2) Make a list of all the things you know about the topic.
3) Find out about the things you need to know. You can go to the library, use the Internet, ask an expert. Make notes.
4) Organise your information: plan, using headings or a web.
5) Use your notes to write your explanation. You can add diagrams, labels, illustrations, photographs, charts, tables or graphs to make your explanation clearer.

Report

1) Choose a topic. Make a list of all the things you know about the topic.
2) Write down the things you need to find out.
3) Find out about the things you need to know. You can go to the library, use the Internet, ask an expert. Make notes.
4) Organise your information: plan, using headings or a web.
5) Start with the most important facts, add some more. You can add diagrams, labels, illustrations, photographs, charts, tables or graphs.

Narrative

1) Write an introduction. (*Who is the story about? Where is the story set? When did the story happen?*)
2) Write about the problem.
3) Write about the solution.
4) Write a conclusion.

Persuasive Argument

1) Write a statement.
2) Give an opinion.
3) Give some reasons why your opinion is important.
4) Write a solution.

When writing for students at this stage:

- Refer to the targets that you wish to focus on and the structure and framework of the text form.
- Explain to the students **why** you are writing, **who** you are writing for, **what** you are going to write about and what text form you are going to use.
- Plan your writing if necessary and appropriate.
- Write in front of the students, demonstrating and talking about what you are doing and how you are applying the structure of the text form. For some text forms, e.g., narrative, this may need to be done in several sessions. Or you might have a draft piece of writing already completed to work on with the students.
- Reread your writing.
- Discuss with the students the message of the writing, encouraging them to think critically about it.
- Refer again to the text form cards and check that the framework is recognisable in the writing.
- Encourage the students to think of things that could be added to the writing or things that could be deleted.
- Use a thesaurus if necessary to find better words.
- Focus the students' attention on the punctuation. Look for places where punctuation has been omitted or needs to be added. Show the students how this is done, using a different coloured pen.
- Focus the students' attention on the spelling. Locate approximated spellings and underline these. Use a dictionary to find the conventional spelling. Write the conventional spelling above the misuse.
- Encourage the students to think critically about the writing, ask questions or make comments.
- Decide on a title for the writing if a title is appropriate.
- Discuss how the writing could be presented in its final form.

3. Writing by Students — Independent Writing

Students need opportunities each day to write by themselves. Providing these opportunities, however, requires careful organisation. In order to give quality teaching time to the students, it is suggested that teachers conference with only one group per day.

There is no one right way to organise students for writing. The organisation in each class will depend on the developmental stage of the students and the number of students in the class. This will differ from class to class.

The following are some suggested approaches.

Note: Class size 25.

Emergent Stage

Three coloured-coded groups (8 per group).

		Monday	Tuesday	Wednesday	Thursday
Red	Daily Demonstrations	Writing Conferencing Spelling Box Activities ⟶	Publishing	Writing	Writing
Blue		Writing Spelling Box Activities ⟶	Writing Conferencing	Publishing	Writing
Green		Writing Spelling Box Activities ⟶	Writing	Writing Conferencing	Publishing

Note: Refer to the spelling section (pages 85–96) for activities the students could be engaged in.

Emergent/Early (1)

Organisation for colour-coded groups.

	Monday		Tuesday	Wednesday	Thursday
Red	T. Demonstration	Writing / Spelling Box Activities	Writing / Conferencing	Publishing	Writing
Blue	Writing / Conferencing / Spelling Box Activities		Publishing	T. Demonstration / Writing	Writing
Green	Writing / Spelling Box Activities		T. Demonstration / Writing	Writing / Conferencing	Publishing

Organisation for Writing at Later Stages of Development

As the students' writing develops, a different organisation is introduced. The following are some examples:

Early (2)/Fluency (1)

Example 1

A Choose a topic to write on.
  Think about why you are writing.
  Think about your planning page.
  Make a sketch plan of the main things you are going to write about quickly.
  Start writing.
B Read your writing to yourself or a partner.
C Proofread your writing.
  - Put a line under your spelling errors.
  - Can you find some words in the dictionary?
D Go back to A.

Example 2

A Choose a topic to write on.
  Think about why you are writing.
  Think about your planning page.
  Make a sketch plan of the main things you are going to write about quickly.
  Start writing.
B Read your writing to yourself or a partner.
C Proofread your writing.
  - Can you add anything?
  - Can you take anything out?
  - Check your punctuation.
  - Underline your spelling errors.
  - Use the dictionary to find the right spelling.
D Go back to A.

Fluency (2)

A Ask yourself:
- What am I going to write about?
- Why am I doing this writing?
- Who am I writing for?
- What text form am I going to use?
- What do I want my readers to know?

B Plan your writing (if necessary).

C Draft your writing.

D Ask yourself:
- Have I said all that I wanted to say?
- Is there anything I should take out?
- Is there anything I should add?
- Can I use any better words?
- Does my writing have the characteristics and framework of the text form I have chosen?

E Ask yourself:
- Have I used correct punctuation?
- Are there any words I need to check for spelling?
- Have I left out any words?

F Share your writing with a partner.

Conferences

Conferences are a very important part of the writing process, as they give feedback to the writer and focus on strengths and needs.

Conferences can take different forms. The following are suggestions for conferences that need to take place within the writing programme.

Partner Conferences

Give each student a partner to read their writing to. The format for the partner conference could be as follows:

- Listen to your partner read their writing.
- Tell your partner what you think the writing is about.
- Ask your partner questions about anything you don't understand. You can use the words *how*, *why*, *when*, *where* and *what*.
- Talk about something in the writing that you liked. (Give your partner a reason.)

Group Conferences

This type of conferencing works best with students once they have reached the beginning of the Fluency stage. When the students have finished a first draft of their writing, they put their names on a chart or whiteboard. Once there are three or four names on the board, the teacher can call a group conference.

The format for the group conference could be as follows:

- The teacher prepares a conference sheet, which includes columns headed "Strengths" and "Needs".
- The writer reads his/her writing to the other students in the group.
- The students take turns around the group giving feedback to the writer about particular strengths of the writing.
- The teacher selects appropriate comments and writes them on the prepared sheet in the column headed "Strengths".
- The students now give comments to the writer about any way they think the writing could be improved.
- The teacher selects appropriate comments and writes them on the prepared sheet in the column headed "Needs".
- The next writer reads his/her writing and the format is repeated.
- The writers continue to work on their writing.

Teacher/Student Conferences

The teacher/student conference varies, depending on the stage of writing development.

At the Emergent/Early stage of writing, the format for the conference could be as follows:

- The teacher talks to the student about planning and makes a positive comment.
- The teacher asks the student either to read the writing or tell about it.
- The teacher makes a comment about the message of the writing.
- At the Emergent stage, the teacher writes the correctly spelled message in a chunk, underneath the student's writing. At the Early stage, once the students are missing lines, the teacher writes words that need correcting on the line above the student's attempt.
- The teacher refers to the goal chart in the back of the student's writing book and gives the student a goal.

Examples of Goal Charts

I CAN ...					
Write letters					
Leave spaces					
Write some whole words					
Have a topic					
Write about something I know					
Make a plan					
Label my plan					

I CAN ...					
Write beginning and end sounds of words					
Write some whole words					
Write a title					
Put a full stop in the right place					
Put a capital letter in the right place					
Write one sentence					
Write two sentences					
Write three sentences					

I CAN ...						
Use some spelling patterns						
Write a title						
Talk about who my audience is						
Write four or more sentences						
Write sentences with different beginnings						
Write a personal experience						
Write to explain something						
Write to describe something						
Write to give an opinion						
Sequence my ideas						
Edit my work by:	adding full stops					
	adding capital letters					
	underlining errors					
	using a dictionary					

At the Fluency stage of writing the student/teacher conference may follow this format:

- The writer reads the writing.
- The teacher comments on the message of the writing.
- The teacher reinforces the strengths of the writing to the writer.
- The teacher and the student discuss needs.
- The teacher selects a teaching point — message, punctuation, spelling.
- The teacher records one or two goals only on the bottom of the student's writing.

Writer Feedback

It is valuable to make time for the students to give feedback about each other's writing. This can be done in a whole class format or a partner format.

Whole Class Feedback

This is a sharing time, usually placed at the end of the writing block, when students who have a published piece of writing share this with the class. If a student is an Emergent reader, it may be appropriate for the teacher to read the writing to the class.

The class is encouraged to give positive comments about the message of the writing or ask the writer a question.

Partner Feedback

As above, but with partners instead of the whole class.

Publishing

Publishing gives a purpose to the writing and is an important factor in keeping students enthusiastic about their writing. Publishing varies at the different stages of a student's writing.

Publishing: Emergent

Publishing: Fluency

Slowly the crocodile approaches the pond looking closely at his prey, a tree snake.

Silently he slips under the water not even making the slightest ripple.

He looks bloodthirstily at his prey then he disappears under the shiny surface. The crocodile appears right under his dinner and gets ready for the pounce. Then, wham, the teeth of the crocodile sink into the snake like the carving knife into the roast.

Suggested Publishing Format

Emergent/Early Stage Publish 1 piece of writing per week	• Teacher publishes the student's writing. • Student illustrates the writing. • Student takes the published writing home to share. • Published writing is glued into the student's large personal scrapbook. • Scrapbook becomes an independent reading centre in the classroom.
Fluency Stage Publish 1 out of 8–10 pieces of writing	• Either the student uses a word processor to enter the writing and the teacher corrects the final form, or the teacher, teacher aid or parent publishes the writing. • Student illustrates the final copy and designs a cover. • A response sheet is glued in the back of the published writing. **Reader's Response Sheet** | Reader's Name	Comment
Mrs E	I liked the way you described the crocodile getting ready for the pounce.
Dad	I felt really sorry for the tree snake. | • Student takes the writing home to share and gather reader responses. • Published writing becomes part of the independent reading in the classroom and other students are encouraged to respond to the messages on the response sheet.

Writing Block Agenda

	Monday–Thursday (approximate time 1 hour)
Block 1	Either a) "writing for" groups of students at similar developmental stage b) "writing with" a group of students at similar developmental stage (shared or interactive writing) c) "writing with" whole class (shared writing). **Note:** If writing for a group, other students would have moved to Block 2.

Block 2	Students would be either:
	    writing independently
	    publishing
	    conferencing.

Block 3	Sharing time.

The emphasis for writing in the first three years of schooling (Years 1–3) should be on learning to write, not on learning text forms or genres.

As students come to understand the process of writing, the structures and features of the different text forms can be introduced to them. The introduction of these text forms should come through guided reading.

The following are different forms of writing that can be introduced when appropriate:

> Thank you notes Postcards Friendly letters Formal letters
> Diaries Journals Personal recounts
> Narratives Adventure stories Mysteries Science fiction
> Fantasy Myths and legends Fables Fairy tales
> Free verse poetry Plays
> Emails Faxes
> Lists Menus Forms
> Procedurals — How to make, to do, to use, to find, recipes, directions, manuals, rules, experiments
> Explanations — explanations across the curriculum, news articles
> Reports — newspaper reports, factual descriptions, glossaries, journals, interviews
> Persuasive arguments — advertisements, letters of complaint, letters to the editor, case pleading, brochures

SPELLING PROGRAMME

Learning to spell is a developmental process. It involves working out the patterns and systems of the English language, then applying these understandings to new words.

A spelling programme should contain activities to develop and practise an understanding of:

- phonic knowledge
- phonemic awareness
- auditory patterns
- orthographic patterns (the spelling patterns that represent sounds in words)
- morphological knowledge (rules and conventions that underlie conventional spelling patterns)
- word sources

In order to keep the spelling programme consistent with the other language programmes described in this book, the stages of spelling will be described as Emergent, Early or Fluency.

OVERVIEW OF THE SPELLING PROGRAMME

Emergent Stage (Level 1)

Teacher Targets	Methods
To establish a print-rich environment.	By labelling, classroom signs, captions, language chunks.
To provide opportunities for students to write daily.	By having a writing block of time each day.
To encourage students to take risks.	By accepting approximations and praising spelling attempts.
To help students to hear sounds in words.	By using an alphabet cue card in writing demonstrations.
To help students segment spoken words into sounds.	By using a variety of pictures, objects etc. for students to respond to in phonemes.
To help students represent the sounds heard in words.	By demonstrations in writing and students' individual writing practice.
To help students to recognise similarities in letters and words.	By matching letter pairs or word pairs. By introducing students to some word families.
To teach students the names of all consonants.	By using alphabet cue cards; through reading and writing components.
To teach students the sound of all initial consonants.	By using alphabet cue cards and books; through reading and writing components. By sorting words according to their beginning sound.
To teach students how each consonant is formed.	By visual language (handwriting) lessons.
To recognise words that rhyme.	By exposing students to poetry. By changing the first sound in a word.

LINKING THE LANGUAGE STRANDS | NEW REVISED EDITION

Student Targets
Students should:
Approximate the spelling of words.
Write the first consonant of a word.
Recognise the difference between a letter and a word.
See similarities in some words and match letters and words.
Know the names of all consonants and vowels.
Know the sound represented by all initial consonants and vowels.
Change the first sound of a word and make a new word (word families: e.g., *cat, bat, sat, rat, hat, fat; look, book, took*).
Recognise words that rhyme.
Hear the phonemes in words and say them.
Clap the sound patterns in words.
Know how to form all letters.
Begin to build a bank of simple high-frequency words that they can write automatically.
Approximate Age Band 4–5 years

Example of Spelling, Emergent Stage (Level 1)

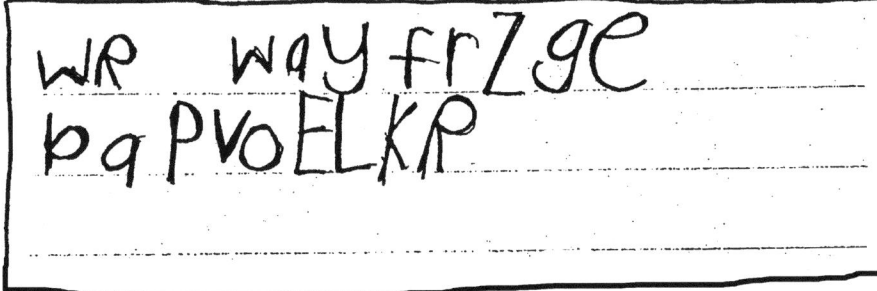

Early Stage (Level 1/2)

Teacher Targets	Methods
To continue to establish a print-rich environment.	By labelling, language chunks, signs.
To continue to provide opportunities for students to write daily.	By having a writing block time.
To encourage students to recognise words that are incorrectly spelled.	By demonstrating how to underline errors in writing.
To teach students how to use the dictionary.	By using alphabet word cards to teach dictionary order. By playing dictionary games.
To encourage students to generate alternative spellings in order to select the right one.	By trying different spellings.
To encourage students to use new words to increase vocabulary.	By focusing on enriching vocabulary in all reading and writing components.
To continue to explore sound and symbol relationships.	By collecting words according to the visual pattern and grouping them. By finding words within words, collecting words that spell a different word when reversed. By playing games such as Hangman. By providing word-sorting activities, e.g., initial letters, common sounds, letter patterns, word families.
To teach students consonant blends and digraphs in initial and final positions.	By using blend and digraph cue cards, books and through all reading and writing components.
To encourage students to learn the conventional spelling of words they can almost spell.	By helping students to begin a word bank, recording words to be learned.
To teach students different ways to learn a word.	By using magnetic letters, letter cards, Scrabble letters etc. to form and reform the word, focusing on its visual pattern.
To teach students the meanings of words and their derivations.	By focusing on vocabulary as it arises in reading and writing components.
To teach students word parts, e.g., compound words and suffixes *-s, -ed, -ing*.	By locating these in reading and writing components and discussing them.

LINKING THE LANGUAGE STRANDS | NEW REVISED EDITION

Student Targets

Students should:

Represent, when writing, all vowel and consonant sounds.

Have an increased bank of known words that are used in writing.

Know ways to learn the correct spelling of a word.

Locate most approximations in writing by underlining them.

Use a dictionary as a word source.

Recognise all consonant blend sounds in initial and final positions.

Recognise all digraphs in initial and final positions.

Recognise long and short vowel sounds.

Recognise vowel and consonant clusters, e.g., *ash, ull, ook, ike*.

Recognise compound words.

Recognise and use suffixes, e.g., *-s, -ed, -ing*.

Use new words that reflect an understanding of their meaning.

Sort words into many different categories.

Recognise word families, e.g., *cake, bake, make, take*.

Approximate Age Band 6-7 years

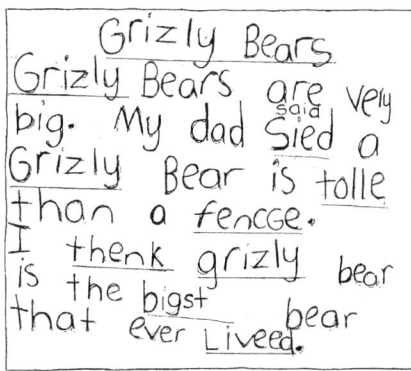

Example of draft writing with student-underlined errors.

A	B	C	D	E	F	G	H	I	J	K	L	M
											lived	
N	O	P	Q	R	S	T	U	V	W	X	Y	Z
					said	think						

Words that the student can almost spell are put in a word bank (see page 94).

Fluency Stage (Level 2/3)

Teacher Targets	Methods
To continue to provide a print-rich environment.	By labelling, language chunks, vocabulary.
To continue to provide opportunities for students to write daily.	By having a writing block of time.
To encourage understanding of the social importance of spelling.	By reinforcing proofreading skills and making sure all published work is correct.
To continue to encourage students to use an increasingly wide vocabulary.	By focusing on enriching vocabulary in all reading and writing components.
To increase students' knowledge of the dictionary and to reinforce dictionary skills.	By demonstrating, by dictionary games and by practice.
To introduce students to a thesaurus and teach its use.	By demonstrating and by practice.
To reinforce a variety of strategies for spelling an unknown word and remembering the correct spelling of difficult words.	By focusing students' attention on sound sequence, knowledge of graphophonic relationships, visual patterns and meaning.
To teach students: • short and long vowel sounds • prefixes • suffixes: *-ly, -ous, -tain, -ful, -ment, -er, -es* • singulars • plurals • base words • synonyms • tenses • antonyms • onomatopoeia • abbreviations • homonyms • silent letters.	By focusing on them as they arise in all language components.
To continue to increase students' knowledge of word families, e.g., *table, cable, able, gable*; *thick, stick, brick*.	By establishing a specific weekly focus and reinforcing word families as they arise in all language components.
To continue to increase students' knowledge of word derivations.	By using word sources to discover and confirm origin, e.g., dictionary, thesaurus.
To continue to increase students' awareness of skills and generalisations.	By discussing these as they arise in all language components.

Student Targets

Students should:

Use a dictionary and thesaurus correctly.

Proofread and correct misuses.

Use a variety of strategies for solving unknown words.

Have a developing spelling conscience.

Have a large bank of words that are spelled correctly in initial drafts.

Use with understanding an increasingly wide vocabulary.

Recognise and use correctly suffixes *-ly, -ous, -tain, -ful, -ment, -er, -es, -est*.

Understand singular, plural and tenses.

Recognise silent letters.

Have an understanding of the terms:
- abbreviation
- antonym
- homonym
- synonym
- base word
- acronym
- onomatopoeia.

Have an increasing understanding of word families, e.g., *thrown, grown, mown*.

Have an increasing understanding of the derivation of words.

Have an increasing understanding of spelling generalisations, e.g., changing *y* to *i* to add an ending, doubling the consonant after a short vowel.

Approximate Age Band 8–10+ years

ORGANISATION AND MANAGEMENT OF THE SPELLING PROGRAMME

The organisation and management of the spelling programme can fall into two parts:

1. Contextual spelling generated through all reading and writing components.
2. Explicit spelling focus.

1. Contextual Spelling

Most of the spelling targets in the previous pages can be introduced, reinforced and practised through the components of reading and writing — shared reading, guided reading, writing for students, writing with students.

It is important to know these targets and to focus the students' attention on them as they arise in natural contexts. They will need continual reinforcement throughout the day, week and year.

2. Explicit Spelling

Some of the targets in the previous pages should be practised in an explicit way.

a) Phonic Knowledge: Letter Name and Sounds (Emergent and Early)

Practise letter names and sounds and blends by saying chants or raps using the sounds. Use alphabet and blend cards, books, tapes etc.

Suggested time — five minutes daily.

Note: This is also integrated with reading and writing programmes, as described above.

b) Phoneme Practice

Have a bag of objects, plastic animals, pictures etc. Hold up something from the bag and encourage the students to say the phonemes they hear in the name of the object.

Use poems, jingles, rhymes, songs and word games.

Suggested time — five minutes daily.

c) Word Families (Emergent, Early and Fluency)

Each week, select a word family to focus on, e.g., *-eam: scream, team, dream, beam*. Add new words to the family as they arise during the week. Take five minutes daily to reinforce these words orally and visually.

d) Word Power

Once a week, allow a 10-minute slot of time for word power. Get the students to write as many words as they can on their own without referring to any word source. Later, tally up the words correctly spelled and write the number on the page.

The next week, repeat the procedure, encouraging the students to increase their number of correctly spelled words. As the students become more proficient spellers, set rules, such as including words with more than three or four letters, words with suffixes and prefixes, word families, etc.

Example of Word Power

Michael - Age 6

September   **October**

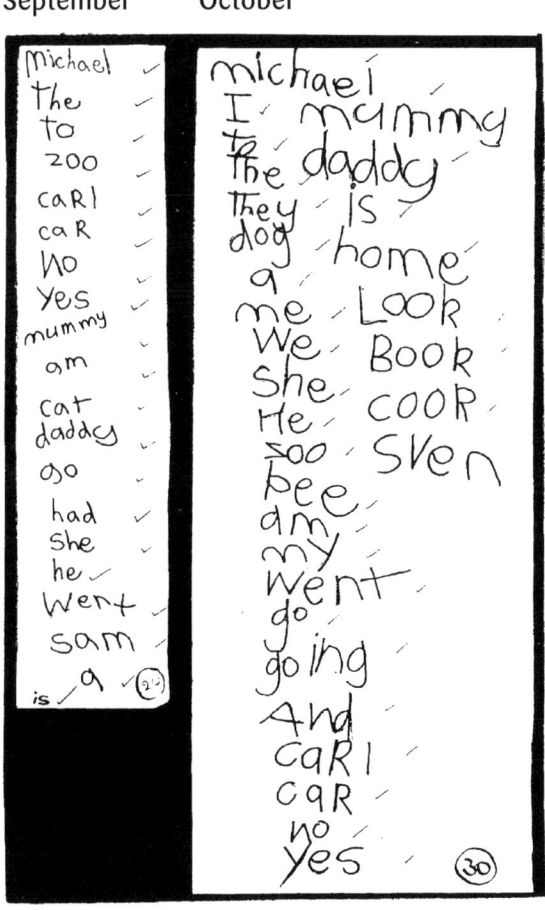

e) Word Bank (Early)

When students reach the Early stage of writing and they are able to spell many high-frequency words correctly, provide them with an individual word bank.

Example

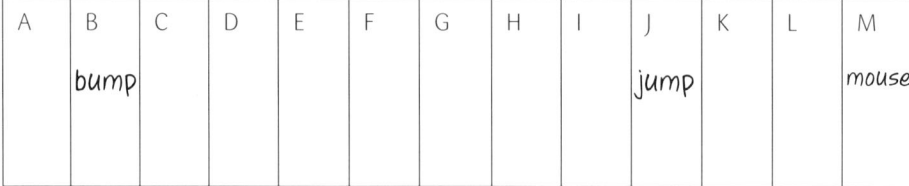

A	B	C	D	E	F	G	H	I	J	K	L	M
	bump								jump			mouse

In writing conferences with students, select words from their writing that they can almost spell and record these in their word banks.

This bank of words is built up over time and is a continual focus. Students are:

- encouraged to take the word bank home each night so that time can be spent on these words at home
- given opportunities during the week to practise the conventional spelling of these words.

The ways in which students learn correct spellings vary with individuals, but the following word bank activities will provide some suggestions.

Word Bank Activities

What can you do?
- Write the words in different ways on the whiteboard.
- Cut the letters of the words out of magazines and paste them onto paper.
- Use letter cards to make the words.
- Use magnetic letters to write the words.
- Make the words out of dough.
- Find each word in the dictionary and write down the page number. What word comes before? What word comes after?
- Put the words into groups:
  - word families
  - rhyming words
  - words with suffixes
  - words with blends.
- Use sponge letters and paint to make the words.
- Type the words on the computer in different fonts and styles.
- Write the words on paper in as many different ways as you can: big, small, wiggly, sideways, skinny, fat.

f) Dictionary Skills (Early and Fluency)

Introduce the students to dictionary skills by initially using an alphabet cue card to practise dictionary order. Focusing on the alphabet card, ask the students questions such as: *What is the first letter in the alphabet? What is the last letter? What are some of the middle letters? What is the letter between* M *and* O*? What is the letter straight after* D*?*

Use the dictionary to play dictionary games, e.g., *Find the middle of the dictionary. Where would you look in the dictionary for the word* **dad** *— the beginning, the middle or the end?*

Suggested time — 10 minutes weekly.

At the Fluency stage, extend the students' understanding of the dictionary by using it to retrieve information on word meaning, derivations, abbreviations, acronyms etc.

g) Individual Conferencing (Early and Fluency)

Conferencing in spelling is usually done as part of the writing conference. During the conference the teacher could:

- praise attempted spellings
- praise efforts to proofread
- check the writing to see if the words already in the word bank have been spelled conventionally
- tick or check the words in pencil if they are correctly spelled
- if the words in the word bank have not been used in writing, quickly check the words by asking the student to write them down for you
- continue to check regularly once the student has mastered the conventional spelling
- put new words that have nearly been spelled correctly into the student's word bank
- examine the spelling of one or two words to see if a common thread emerges, e.g., not doubling the consonant after a short vowel, not changing the *y* to *i* when adding an ending, not recognising some blend sounds
- use this as a teaching point and establish a goal.

Spelling Time

A daily time can be allocated for explicit spelling instruction and independent activities. Activities should be chosen according to the different stages of spelling development.

Emergent Group

Students at this stage could be working on independent or group activities and games that reinforce:

> high-frequency words
>
> consonant names   word families
>
> consonant sounds   rhyming words
>
> vowel names   word/letter differentiation
>
> vowel sounds   similarities/patterns in words

Early Group

Students at this stage could be:

- working with the words in their word banks to learn the correct spelling
- working on independent or group activities/games that reinforce early targets:

> identifying words spelled incorrectly
>
> dictionary skills
>
> blends
>
> long and short vowels
>
> compound words
>
> suffixes: *-s, -ed, -ing*
>
> sorting word categories
>
> word families

Fluency Group

Students at this stage could be:

- working on word bank activities when necessary
- working with individual spelling books (see this page) to record words under the appropriate headings
- working with independent or group activities or games that reinforce Fluency targets:

> using the dictionary
>
> using the thesaurus
>
> proofreading and correcting misuses
>
> suffixes: -*ly*, -*ous*, -*tain*, -*ful*, -*ment*, -*er*, -*en*, -*est*
>
> singular, plural and tenses
>
> silent letters
>
> abbreviations/homonyms/synonyms/base words
>
> word families
>
> word origins

Spelling Book

The spelling book is introduced for students at the Fluency stage. It is a blank book in which students glue pages with headings such as: happy words, sad words, angry words, scary words, funny words, synonyms, homonyms, antonyms, word derivations, suffixes, plurals, personal thesaurus, spelling conventions.

The students collect words and categorise them accordingly.

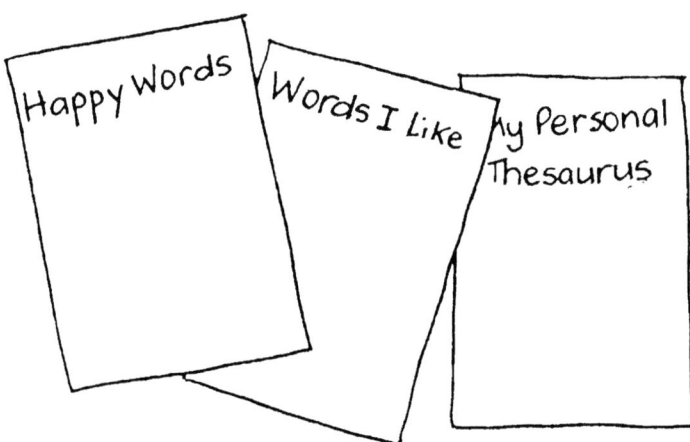

VISUAL LANGUAGE PROGRAMME

The strand of visual language is divided into two sub-strands:

1. **Viewing**

2. **Presenting**

SUGGESTED LEARNING OUTCOMES

1. Viewing
- To explore the use of a variety of visual techniques to present information.
- To explore the technical features of visual presentations,
  e.g., headings, point size, fonts, graphics, shading.
- To use the language associated with visual media when viewing formats,
  e.g., layout, design, font, gutter, page layout, graphics.
- To understand that written and visual components work together,
  e.g., advertisements, posters, diagrams.
- To view a variety of formats as a source of information,
  e.g., advertisements, posters, graphs, diagrams, charts.
- To experience verbal and non-verbal features of language,
  e.g., mime, drama, play performances.
- To view photography and film and discuss interpreted meanings.

2. Presenting
- To be able to form letters and numerals in a legible way.
- To be aware of print media formats, e.g., posters, advertisements.
- To be able to make presentations using a variety of formats,
  e.g., posters, advertisements, charts, diagrams.
- To use language associated with presented formats,
  e.g., design, layout, font, gutter, margin.
- To be familiar with the technology available for publication of texts,
  e.g., computers, photocopiers.
- To be able to use techniques to present information,
  e.g., fonts, colour, graphics.
- To make presentations using moving imagery,
  e.g., mime, drama, plays, performances.
- To present information using photography and film.

Examples of Presenting Information in Different Ways

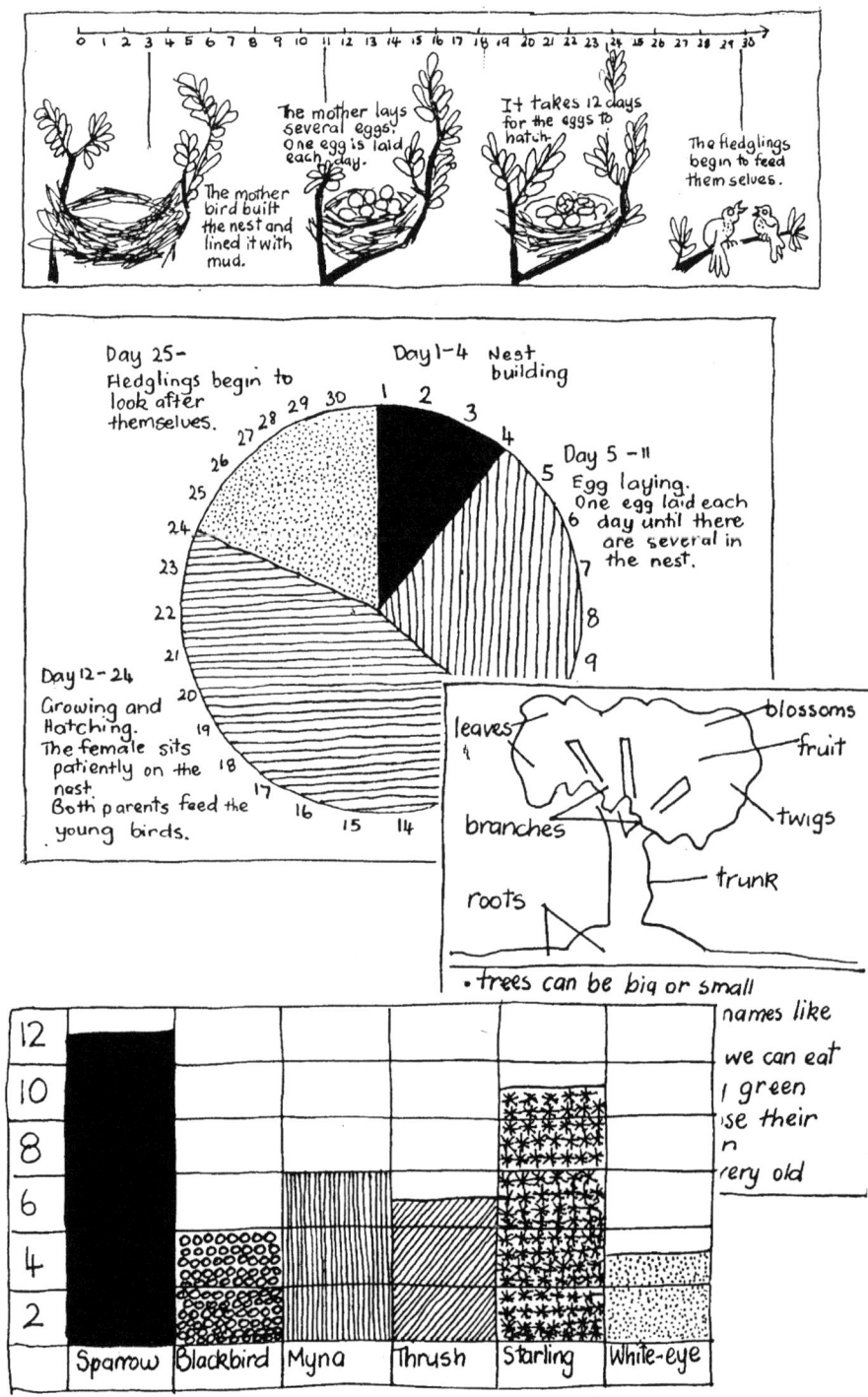

OVERVIEW OF THE VISUAL LANGUAGE PROGRAMME

1. Viewing

Teacher Targets	Methods
To provide a programme that allows the students to view a variety of visual features.	By experiencing a variety of presentations in all curriculum areas.
To provide opportunities to view and discuss static and moving imagery as a source of information.	By viewing presentations such as charts, diagrams, role-play, drama, video and film.
To provide opportunities to view the features of printed material.	By using magazines, newspapers, books and other printed material that show a variety of visual features.
To expose students to the link between verbal and visual language.	By giving students opportunities to view visual language and discuss meaning.
To expose students to the language associated with visual presentations.	By discussing a variety of visual presentations using appropriate language.
To encourage students to experience the verbal and non-verbal features of language.	By comparing (e.g., plays and performances) and understanding the differences between verbal and non-verbal components.

Student Targets

These are the specific achievement objectives.

Emergent Stage (Level 1)	Early Stage (Level 1/2)	Fluency Stage (Level 2/3)
Students should:	*Students should:*	*Students should:*
View creative presentations that use a variety of techniques, e.g., crayon and dye, painting.	View creative presentations that use a variety of techniques, e.g., collage, printing.	View creative presentations that use a variety of techniques, e.g., pencil sketching, sculptures, carvings.
View functional presentations using a variety of formats, e.g., diagrams, labels, index.	View functional presentations that use a variety of formats, e.g., diagrams, maps, plans, index.	View functional presentations that use a variety of formats, e.g., time lines, graphs, cross-sections.
View books and talk about their features, e.g., print size, changes in font, title size.	View a variety of printed material, e.g., posters, charts, and discuss print size, font, colour, design.	View a variety of printed material, e.g., advertisements, scripts, brochures; discuss design and layout.
View illustrations, photographs and discuss their meaning.	View and compare illustrations and photographs; discuss meaning.	View illustrations and photographs and analyse and evaluate the way the visual features are organised and combined for different meaning, effects, purposes.
View plays and performances and talk about their visual components, e.g., characters, props, body language; talk about message.	View plays and performances and discuss visual components, e.g., props, characters, body language; discuss message.	View plays, performances, videos and films and describe how verbal and visual features are combined for different purposes and audiences.
Approximate Age Band 4-5 years	Approximate Age Band 5-7 years	Approximate Age Band 8-10+ years

2. Presenting

Teacher Targets	Methods
To provide a programme that allows students to present in a variety of ways.	By regular opportunities to practise presenting in all curriculum areas.
To provide experience in making static images.	By giving regular opportunities to present information in both creative (painting/drawings) and functional (diagrams, graphs) forms.
To provide experience in creating moving imagery.	By giving experiences in role-play and drama.
To provide opportunities to use a range of technology for presentations.	By using current technology available, e.g., computer, overhead projector, photocopier.
To increase students' vocabulary to include language associated with visual features.	By using appropriate visual language when presenting.
To form letters and numerals legibly.	By providing practice and support according to stages of development.
To develop a functional pencil-holding grip.	By providing regular practice, adjusting grip where necessary.

Student Targets

These are specific achievement objectives.

Emergent Stage (Level 1)	Early Stage (Level 1/2)	Fluency Stage (Level 2/3)
Students should:	*Students should:*	*Students should:*
Make creative presentations using simple techniques, e.g., crayon, dye and paint.	Make creative presentations using a variety of techniques, e.g., crayon, dye, Indian ink, collage, batik.	Make creative presentations using a variety of more complex techniques, e.g., clay, sketching, mixed media, and using appropriate language.
Make functional presentations using simple formats, e.g., diagrams, labels.	Make functional presentations using a variety of formats, e.g., maps, trails and charts.	Make functional presentations using a variety of more complex techniques, e.g., graphs, time lines, brochures, advertisements, and using appropriate language.
Begin to know the starting point and direction when forming letters and numerals.	Begin to use technology when making visual presentations, e.g., computer.	Use a range of technology when presenting visual information, e.g., computer, overhead projector.
Begin to develop a functional pencil-holding grip.	Make upper and lower case letters uniform in size and in appropriate line position.	Write legibly.
Perform simple role plays.	Use a functional pencil-holding grip.	Link letters.
	Begin to demonstrate consistency of size, shape, slope and spacing.	Write with fluency of movement.
	Perform role-plays and mimes.	Perform mime, drama and plays to a variety of audiences.
Approximate Age Band 4-5 years	**Approximate Age Band 6-7 years**	**Approximate Age Band 8-10+ years**

ORGANISATION AND MANAGEMENT OF THE VISUAL LANGUAGE PROGRAMME

The number of visual images that surround us are immeasurable. Through such media as television, advertisements and the printed word, visual messages often dominate students' lives.

Opportunities arise in many curriculum areas to incorporate this strand. Research has shown that:

- communication through visual images is probably the most efficient means of conveying meaning
- a visual image has the ability to convey meaning at a glance
- a visual image can convey more than a verbal message. A verbal message often requires intellectual attention to achieve the same level of communication
- students' memories for images appear to be better than for verbal messages
- visual communication can be a superior means of transmitting information.

Suggestions for Establishing Visual Language

1. Collect a variety of materials that provide examples of visual language.

advertisements	cards	pamphlets	labels
letterheads	flags	articles	notices
calendars	brochures	menus	symbols
invitations	coins	medals	stamps
book covers	signs	postcards	logos
catalogues	weather maps	table mats	disc covers
posters	badges	safety cards	wordless texts

2. Set up a display board and change the visual display frequently.
   Add open questions:

   What do these signs tell us?
   What audience do you think this would be for?
   Why is colour important here?
   What do you think makes this design effective?

Suggestions for Working with Visual Language

Select appropriate points to discuss, using terminology suitable to the developmental stage of the students.

Visual Language — Terminology (samples)

Visual Language	Terminology (samples)
Illustrations Discuss: • features used by the illustrator • how students feel about illustrations • what students think the text will be about • techniques used by the illustrator • a particular illustrator and their approach over a series of text illustrations.	colour technique border graphics gutter bleed keyline
Print Discuss: • a variety of print formats — books, magazines, newspapers • design and layout of the print on the page • use of fonts.	font/typeface page layout column margin left justification right justification centre balance
Advertisements Discuss: • message intended • purpose • selected advertisements • favourite advertisements • importance of words, images, music, main focus • use of stereotypes • heading types • catchphrases • logos.	spacing lettering font/typeface upper/lower case balance colour layout headings audience background

Photography Discuss: • meaning within pictures • images • placement of objects • the scene • colour photography • black and white photographic design — landscape, portrait.	shot composition lighting tone colour horizontal vertical square frame scene
Comic/Cartoon Discuss: • meaning • the illustrator's style • messages within visual images • devices such as framing, speech bubbles • a favourite cartoon • a favourite character • advertisements on television.	flow sequence style layout
Television Discuss: • popular programmes • findings of surveys • time allotments to specific programmes • types of programme • news presentations • frontline presenters • advertisements — messages and intended audiences • TV guides — layout and design.	message programme film media presenters documentaries series
Maps Discuss: • types of map, e.g., road, weather • layout and design • presented information • use of keys • symbols.	layout design key symbol scale legend

Example: Designing a Map

Suggestions for Using Creative Visual Language

Progressive Development

Paint	Paint	Crayon, dye and Indian ink
Crayon	Crayon and dye	Tempera and Indian ink
Dye	Crayon, dye and Indian ink	Indian ink and charcoal
Card and sponge prints	Simple screen prints	Screen prints
	Indian ink and charcoal	Paper collage
	Collage	Batik

Suggestions for Using Functional Visual Language

Simple Diagrams

The purpose of diagrams is to show:

- subjects or concepts visually
- the relationships between the parts of a subject or concept.

Examples

The students can make simple diagrams to show animal groups, body parts, plant parts, working parts.

Beginning	Developing	Competent
Students can: • construct a simple diagram • add labels to key parts of a subject • talk about the information presented on a labelled diagram.	*Students can:* • construct a diagram • add a number of labels relevant to the subject • talk about the information presented on a labelled diagram.	*Students can:* • construct a diagram • add labels to a key part of a diagram • talk and write about the information presented in a diagram.

Flow/Sequence Diagrams

The purpose of flow and sequence diagrams is to:

- define, explain or summarise a process change
- present a set of instructions
- show changes, or cause and effect, over time.

Examples

The students can make flow and sequence diagrams to show processes (such as life cycles, growing plants, hatching eggs), how products and services come to us, how something is made.

Beginning	Developing	Competent
Students can: • construct a simple flow diagram • construct a simple sequence diagram • add labels • talk about information included in a simple flow or sequence diagram.	*Students can:* • construct a flow and sequence diagram to present information • add some written language • use arrows to show directionality • add numerals • talk about information presented in a flow and sequence diagram.	*Students can:* • construct information to form meaningful sequences in flow and sequence diagrams • add precise language • use arrows and numbers to show directionality • talk and write about information presented in flow and sequence diagrams.

Cross-Section/Cutaway Diagrams

The purpose of cross-sections and cutaway diagrams is to:

- explore below the surface of a subject
- show how to assemble the parts of a subject.

Examples

The students can make cross-section and cutaway diagrams to show what is inside engines, clocks, fruit, burrows, beehives, underground train systems, skyscrapers, our bodies, a doll's house.

Beginning	Developing	Competent
Students can: • talk about information presented in a cutaway or a cross-section.	*Students can:* • understand that a subject has an internal structure as well as an external appearance • talk about information presented in a cutaway or a cross-section.	*Students can:* • construct cutaways and cross-sections • add labels and captions to support diagrams • talk and write about information presented in a cutaway and a cross-section.

Maps and Plans

The purpose of maps and plans is to:

- show spatial connections
- locate a subject
- define territories.

Examples

The students can make maps and plans of a bedroom, a house, a neighbourhood, a farm, a town, a city, a country, a system (e.g., rail), an airport, animal cages, unusual buildings.

Beginning	Developing	Competent
Students can: • draw a simple map or plan of a familiar place • add labels • talk about the information on maps or plans.	*Students can:* • draw maps and plans • add labels • add symbols and keys • talk and write about the information on maps and plans.	*Students can:* • draw maps and plans • add labels • add symbols, keys/legends, colour coding, compass bearings • talk and write about the information presented on maps and plans.

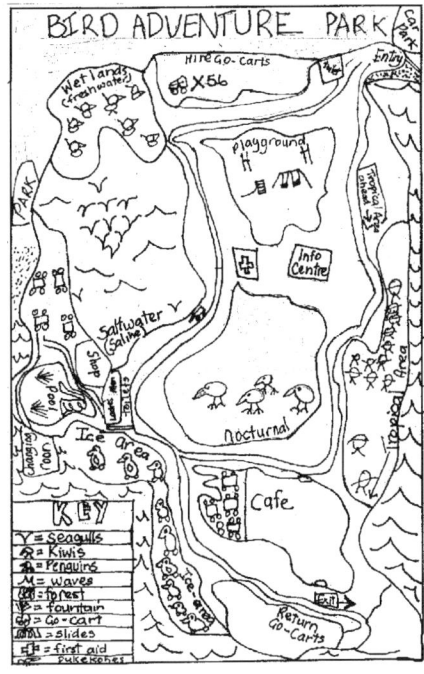

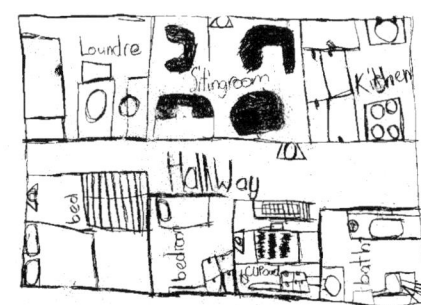

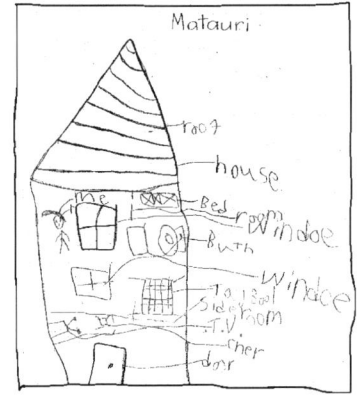

Graphs

The purpose of graphs is to:

- measure and show quantity, height, speed, temperature etc.
- compare and rank information
- summarise or highlight statistical information.

Examples

The students can make graphs and information boxes to classify, group, compare or summarise data and survey results, and to develop such things as rosters, timetables or schedules.

Beginning	Developing	Competent
Students can: • classify information into groups • talk about the information presented in a simple graph.	*Students can:* • construct a simple graph to present information for comparison • construct a bar and pie graph • add numerals • talk about the information presented in a graph.	*Students can:* • talk and write about the information presented in graphs • present information in bar, column, pie and line graphs • add elements such as numerals, headings, co-ordinate points • scan a graph and locate specific information in it.

Time Lines

The purpose of time lines is to:

- make a record of history or a sequence of events
- show facts in chronological order
- summarise growth, change and development
- find patterns and connections in a series or process
- show changes over time.

Examples

The students can make time lines to record prehistoric eras, animal life cycles, changes in a neighbourhood, changes in personal development, growth and historical development.

Beginning	Developing	Competent
Students can: • talk about the information on a simple time line • construct a simple time line to show growth and change.	*Students can:* • construct a time line to show a time sequence • construct a time line that shows growth and change • add some language to a time line • talk about the information presented in time lines.	*Students can:* • talk and write about the information in time lines • present information in a time line that shows growth and change, cause and effect • add language • understand and use a variety of time units, e.g., minutes, hours, years, seasons, centuries • measure elapsed time between events on a time line.

Matauri Age 5

Tables and Informational Boxes

The purpose of tables and informational boxes is to:

- display pictorial or written information/record information, results and findings
- list items for reference
- organise information into groups for comparison and evaluation
- find patterns and correlations in data
- schedule or demonstrate events.

Examples

The students can make tables and informational boxes to classify, group, compare or summarise data and survey results, and to develop such things as rosters, timetables or schedules.

Beginning	Developing	Competent
Students can: • talk about the information presented in a box or simple table.	*Students can:* • talk about the information presented in a box or table • present information in boxes • present information in simple tables • write some text to include in a box/table.	*Students can:* • talk and write about information presented in a box or table • present information in boxes and tables • add concise text to a box/table • understand the function of cells and headings • scan a table and locate specific information in it.

A Visual Strategy to Use in the Classroom

The following is a visual strategy that can be used in conjunction with the writing programme. It can be developed in progressive stages.

A) Interpreting Graphics

- Give the students experience in working with graphics by presenting some information for the class to interpret. The information could be about yourself. Pose a question, e.g., *What can you tell me about my family and where I live?*

- Draw graphics in sequence, allowing time for each idea to be interpreted and extended, e.g., a response to the first graphic might be:

    S: *There are five people in your family.*

    T: *Tell me more.*

    S: *There are five in your family — two adults and three children. There are four males and one female.*

- Give the students time to make a presentation about their family using graphs.

B) Teacher Demonstration

- Gather the students on the teaching space to retell a story using simple graphics. Add labels.

- Engage the students in discussion about the graphics. Encourage the students to think critically. Highlight features of interest, excitement, importance etc. Define starting and ending points (optional).
- Demonstrate a short, well-paced piece of writing, using the graphics.

> It was a very stormy night. The rain poured down. Lightning flashed and thunder crashed. The farmer put on a warm coat, thick hat and waterproof boots. She went out into the cold wet night to check the sheep.

Suggested Stages for Students Using Visual Strategies

Linking to Pre-Writing

Stage 1	Simple visuals representing students' ideas. These are usually based on personal experiences.
Stage 2	Visuals now include labels.
Stage 3	Visuals representing ideas are in sequence. These may include arrows, lines or numerals.
Stage 4	Visual representation is connected to the text form that is being used.

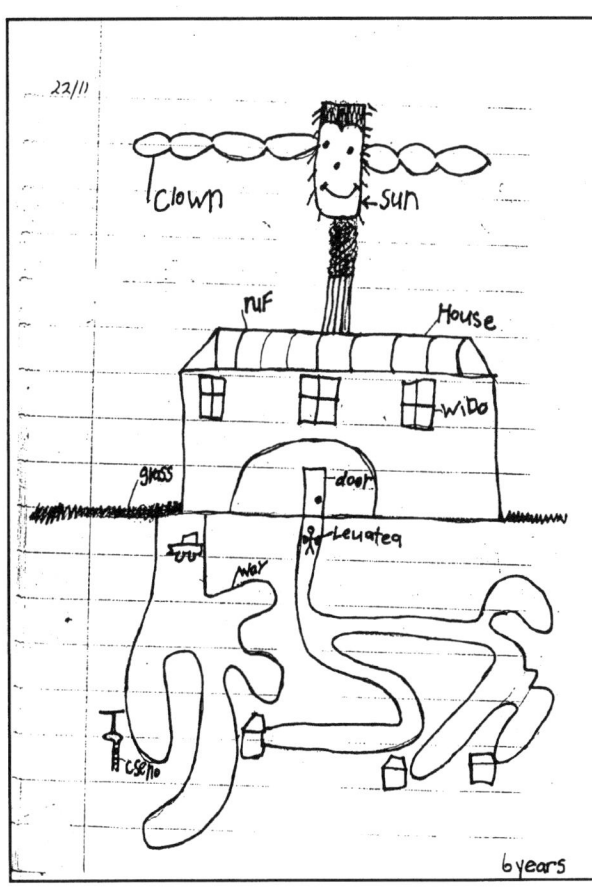

ORGANISATION OF THE CLASSROOM ENVIRONMENT

A key to successful organisation is developing a student-centred environment that is stimulating and purposeful.

Begin with a critical look at the physical environment and consider the following points:

- Do you require everything that is in your room, or can you utilise the space more effectively?
- Do you need a teacher's table, or could you make better use of the space if it was removed?
- How can you divide your classroom into manageable learning spaces?
- In what ways can you make the wall space more visually attractive, as well as being interactive?

Learning Centres or Stations

Establishing learning centres within a classroom setting is an effective way of enhancing students' learning while at the same time giving the teacher time to work with individuals and small groups.

Learning centres provide reinforcement, extension and enrichment of concepts and skills. They move students away from the teacher — from centred learning to independent and responsible learning.

Refer to *Linking the Language Strands Learning Stations* (Wings Publications, PO Box 54163, Bucklands Beach, Auckland) for ideas on independent activities.

SETTING OUT THE CLASSROOM

The following examples show different layouts for the physical space. The setting up of the environment will be determined by the size of the classroom and the number of students who will be using it.

The examples on pages 117–118 suggest layouts for small and large spaces.

Example One: A Small Classroom Space

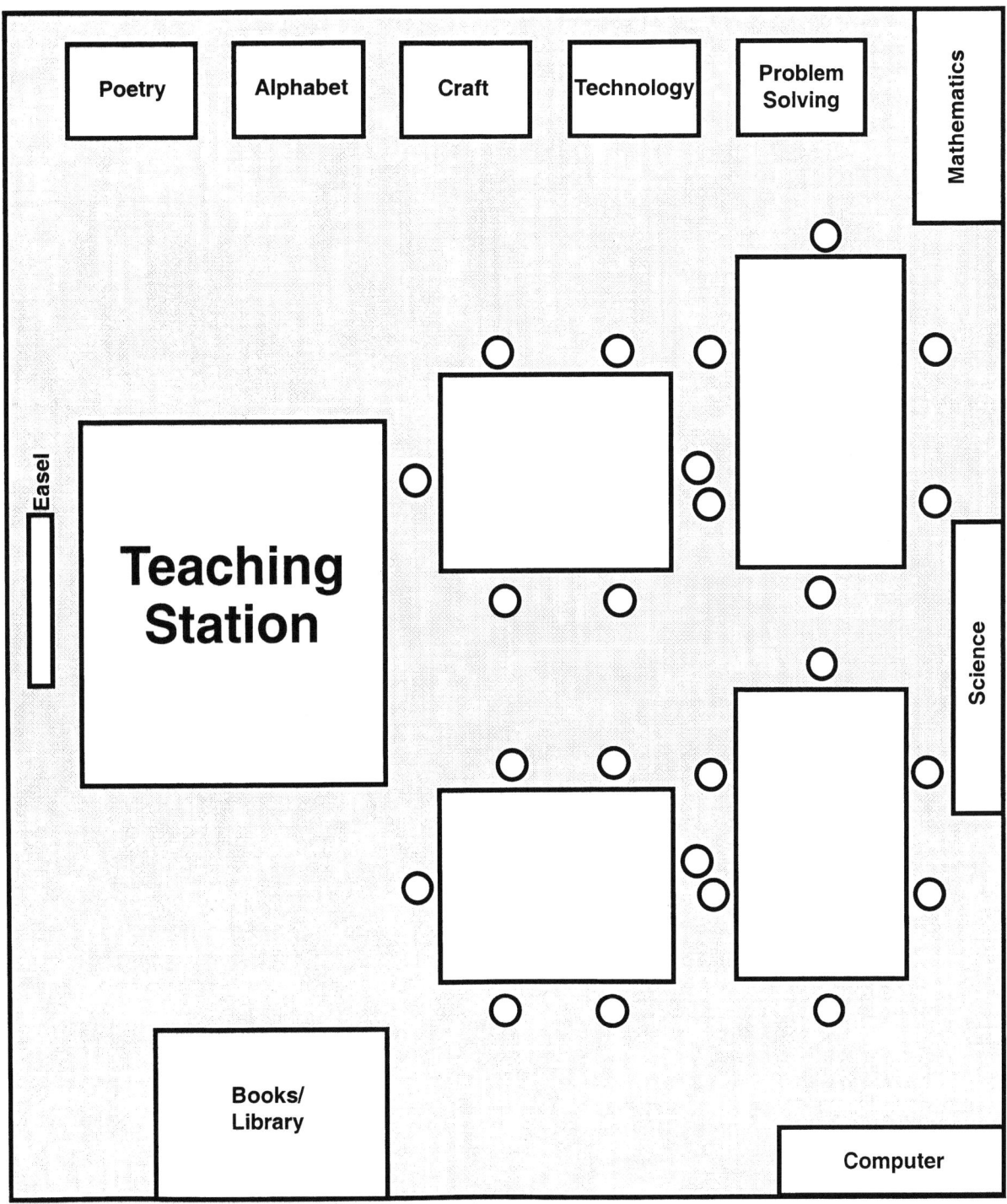

Example Two: A Large Classroom Space

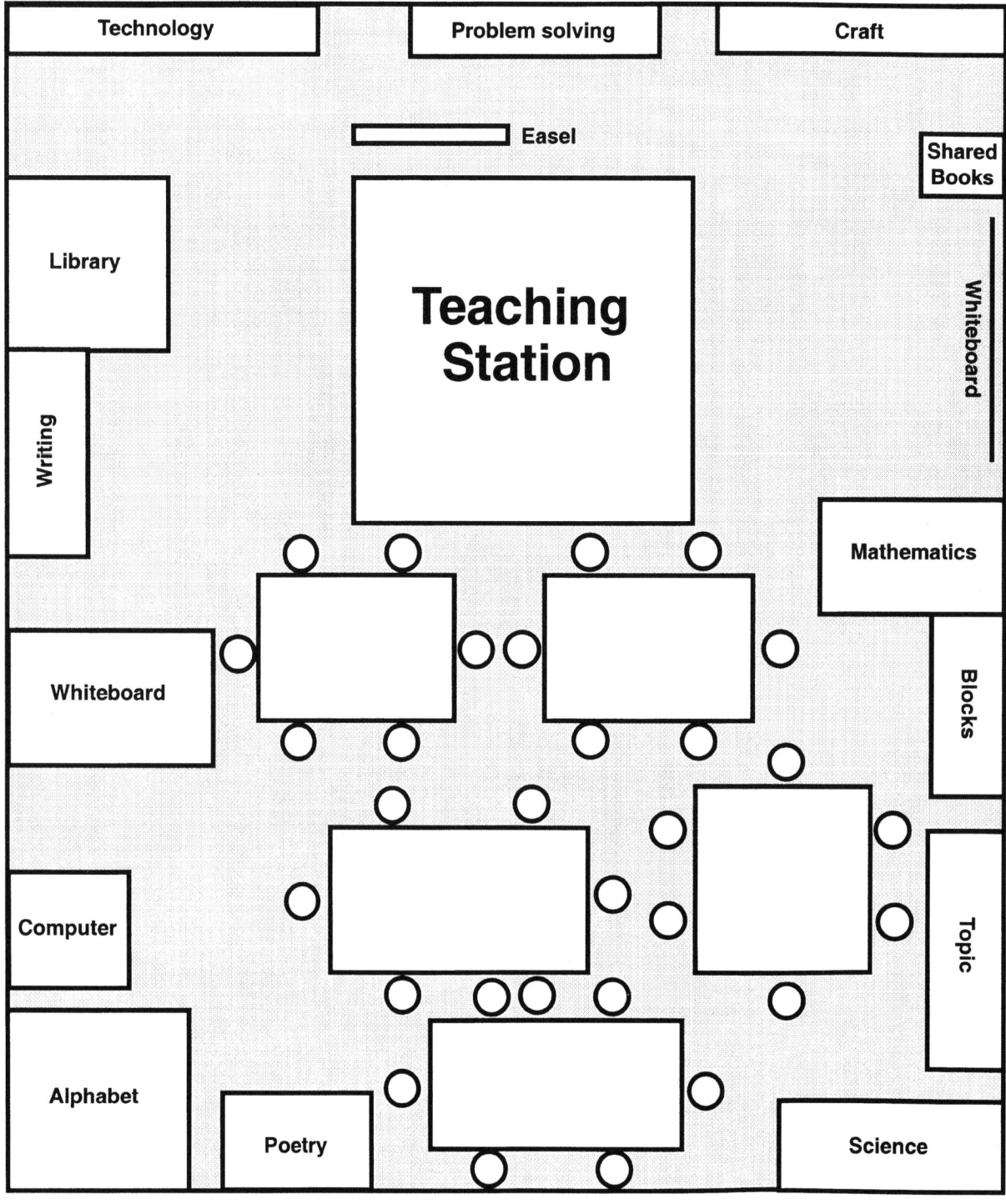

ORGANISATION OF TIME

The successful management of a class programme depends upon the thoughtful organisation of a class or school schedule. A schedule needs to flow smoothly from one block to another, with minimal interruptions.

The following schedule provides blocks of focus time and a balance between active and receptive learning.

Note: This schedule is organised to follow a similar pattern from Monday to Thursday.

Schedule 1	
Monday–Thursday	
Block 1 (30 mins)	Greetings, roll etc. **Oral Language** (10 minutes) **Shared Reading News Book** (10 mins) **Physical Fitness Activities** (10 mins)
Block 2 (1 hour 10 mins)	**Written Language** — Reading (1 hour 10 mins) • shared book • guided reading • independent reading • reading-related learning stations (directed) • sharing time (include reading to)
INTERVAL/RECESS	
Block 3 (1 hour 30 mins)	**Written Language** — Writing (1 hour) • teacher demonstration • students' writing • teacher/student conferencing • spelling activities (independent) • sharing time **Spelling** (20 minutes) • class focus (5 mins) • independent spelling activities (10 mins) • class focus (5 mins) **Shared Reading Poetry** (10 mins)
LUNCH	
Block 4 (1 hour 30 mins)	**Reading to** (15 minutes) **Mathematics** (45 minutes) **Theme Focus** (30 minutes) (One theme taken over 3-4 weeks)

Note: These times are suggested only. Priority is given to vital areas of curriculum learning at this stage of development.

Schedule 2	
Monday–Thursday	
Block 1 (30 mins)	Greetings, roll etc. **Oral Language** (10 minutes) **Shared Reading News Book** (10 mins) **Physical Fitness Activities** (10 mins)
Block 2 (1 hour)	**Mathematics** (50 minutes) **Shared Reading Poetry** (10 mins)
INTERVAL/RECESS	
Block 3 (1 hour 30 mins)	**Written Language** — Writing (1 hour) • teacher demonstration • students' writing • teacher/student conferencing • sharing time **Spelling** (20 minutes) • class focus • independent activities **Reading to**
LUNCH	
Block 4 (1 hour 30 mins)	**Written Language** — Reading (1 hour) • shared reading • guided reading • independent reading • sharing time • reading to **Theme Focus** (30 minutes)

Friday Schedule	
Monday-Thursday	
Block 1 (1 hour 30 mins)	Greetings, roll etc. **Oral Language** — News and Views Book **Shared Book** — Processing
INTERVAL/RECESS	
Block 2 (1 hour 30 mins)	**Poetry Focus** — Processing (30 minutes) **Mathematics** (45 minutes) **Reading to** (15 minutes)
LUNCH	
Block 3 (1 hour 30 mins)	Theme/IT/Library/Assemblies/Sports

Note: Friday timetable could be more flexible within each school's requirements.

CONCLUSION

The three language strands — oral, written and visual — referred to in this book are all equally important and, when used in a balanced programme, they will cater for students' different learning styles.

The careful organisation and management of these language strands is essential to a successful classroom programme.

If sound management and organisation strategies have been put in place, the students will have a greater opportunity to reach their learning potential and become independent, lifelong learners.

REFERENCES

Learning Media Wellington, *English in the New Zealand Curriculum.* Ministry of Education, New Zealand.

Learning Media Wellington, *The Learner As a Reader.* Ministry of Education, New Zealand.

Learning Media Wellington, *Exploring Language.* Ministry of Education, New Zealand.

Learning Media Wellington, *Effective Literacy Practice Years 1 to 4.* Ministry of Education, New Zealand.